Graeme E. Ballantine

AN INTRODUCTION TO WITTGENSTEIN'S TRACTATUS

PHILOSOPHY

Editor
PROFESSOR H. J. PATON
M.A., F.B.A., D.LITT., LL.D.
Emeritus Professor of Moral Philosophy in the University of Oxford

AN INTRODUCTION TO WITTGENSTEIN'S TRACTATUS

G. E. M. ANSCOMBE
Lecturer and Research Fellow of Somerville College, Oxford

HUTCHINSON UNIVERSITY LIBRARY
LONDON

HUTCHINSON & CO. (*Publishers*) LTD
178–202 Great Portland Street, London, W.1

London Melbourne Sydney
Auckland Bombay Toronto
Johannesburg New York

First published 1959
Second edition 1963

This book has been printed in Great Britain by litho-offset by William Clowes and Sons Ltd, London and Beccles, and bound by them

ACKNOWLEDGMENTS

Most of what appears here was originally delivered in the form of lectures at Oxford in the Michaelmas and Hilary Terms, 1957–8. I am indebted, first, to the Oxford audiences who in successive years provided me with the occasion for getting my ideas of the *Tractatus* straight; and, secondly, to Professor Paton, the Editor of this series, who made many useful criticisms of my exposition. I am also much indebted to Peter Geach for help afforded in frequent discussions and in revising the book. In particular, I obtained some logical information and references from him; for example, he supplied me with the explanations given in Chapter 9 of Wittgenstein's criticisms of *Principia Mathematica*, concerning the 'ancestral relation' and the unacknowledged use of 'formal series' made by Russell and Whitehead. Finally, I have had the advantage of reading through Professor Erik Stenius' highly interesting book on the *Tractatus* before its publication. It presents a very different account from my own of some important points, and enabled me to sharpen my own ideas by contrast.

I am grateful to the Rockefeller Foundation, which has supported me during six years' work on Wittgenstein's MSS.; this book was written during my tenure of a Research Fellowship sponsored by the Foundation.

Oxford G. E. M. ANSCOMBE

CONTENTS

FOREWORD

An Introduction to Wittgenstein's Tractatus may seem to differ in character from the books hitherto published in the present philosophical series: it makes a freer use of technical expressions, and it demands a greater effort from the general reader. This is inevitable from the very nature of the subject; for Wittgenstein's thinking sprang from the modern development of mathematical logic; and he makes few concessions to the uninitiated. Indeed, it is for this reason that an introduction to his work is so urgently required; and with its aid the reader who has grasped some elementary techniques of modern logic (which should not prove too difficult) may hope to find his way about in what to many has been a closed field of thought. The opening up of such a field is fully in accord with the general aim of the series, even if the difficulties to be tackled may be greater than usual. It might almost be said, in view of the influence exercised by Wittgenstein, that without an introduction of this kind the aim of the series would be imperfectly realized.

To this it may be objected that the *Tractatus* has now been superseded. In one sense this is true; for its author has expressly recognized that it contains grave mistakes. But the *Tractatus* by no means loses its historical importance because of this frank admission. As a philosophical work begins to recede into history, an attempt to expound its doctrine and estimate its significance may become both more necessary and more easy. Wittgenstein himself was of the opinion that his more recent works could be seen in the right light only by contrast with, and against the background of, his earlier way of thinking. Hence it is my hope that Miss Anscombe's work may serve as an introduction not merely to the *Tractatus*, but also indirectly to his philosophy as a whole.

H. J. PATON

NOTE ON SECOND EDITION

Apart from the correction of some obvious mistakes and misprints, and some other slight improvements of the text, I have taken the opportunity to add a paragraph to the end of Chapter 10 and to change pages 166–7.

G. E. M. ANSCOMBE

INTRODUCTION

Ludwig Wittgenstein was born in Vienna in 1889, the eighth child of a family largely Jewish by extraction, though not by persuasion. His father had started the modern iron and steel industry in Austria; he was a man of forcible character who was generally both much feared and much respected. The children were brought up in an atmosphere of extreme contempt for most kinds of low standard. The whole generation had an unusual fire about them. All were aesthetically and, in particular, musically talented to a high degree; the father, however, though sharing such interests up to a point, regarded them as suited only to be a side-line for his sons: the only fit career for them was civil engineering. (It had to be concealed from him that one of them as a child played the violin in St. Peter's Church in Vienna.) The combination of family temperament and the attitude of the parents—who could not conceive that their children might suffer miseries worth taking account of—led to at least one suicide among the sons. Of himself, Ludwig said: 'I had an unhappy childhood and a most miserable youth'; but again, in connection with the work that a man was content to publish: 'I had luck: I was very well brought up'—i.e. as far as concerned critical standards.

Ludwig came to Manchester at the age of about nineteen to study engineering; but by 1911 his interest had been caught by the philosophy of mathematics, and he went to Cambridge to study under Russell. From 1912 to 1917 he was engaged in writing the work which is the subject of this book. The greater part of the writing was done while he was on active service in the Austrian army.

As a boy of sixteen Wittgenstein had read Schopenhauer and had been greatly impressed by Schopenhauer's theory of the 'world as idea' (though not of the 'world as will'); Schopenhauer then struck him as fundamentally right, if only a few adjustments and clarifications were made. It is very much a popular notion of Wittgenstein that he was a latter-day Hume; but any connections between them are indirect, and he never read more than a few pages of Hume. If we look for Wittgenstein's philosophical ancestry, we should rather look to Schopenhauer; specifically, his 'solipsism', his conception of 'the limit' and his ideas on value will be better understood in the light of Schopenhauer than of any other philosopher. It is one of the oddities of the present day that Schopenhauer is often vaguely associated with Nietzsche and even with Nazism, and is thought to be some kind of immoralist, worshipper of power and praiser of suicide; it is not the mythical Schopenhauer of popular repute, but the actual Schopenhauer, that we should remember in connection with Wittgenstein.

For the rest, Wittgenstein's philosophical influences are pretty well confined to Frege and to Russell, who introduced him to Frege's writings. His relative estimate of them comes out in the acknowledgment he makes in the Preface to the *Tractatus*: 'I owe a great part of the stimulation of my thoughts to the great works of Frege and to the writings of my friend Mr. Bertrand Russell.'

Frege, whose first important work was published in 1879 and who died in 1925, was a philosopher whose greatness, up to the present day, was acknowledged only by a very few. Russell and Wittgenstein were the most eminent of those who recognized it. He was not a general philosopher and had no concern with either ethics or theory of knowledge, but purely with logic and the foundations of mathematics; here however his considerations, being always concerned with fundamentals, are of the greatest general philosophical importance. I devote a good deal of space to Frege in this book for the following reason: Wittgenstein's *Tractatus* has captured the interest and excited the admiration of many, yet almost all that has been published about it has been wildly irrelevant. If this has had any one cause, that cause has been the neglect of Frege and of the new direction that he gave to philosophy. In the *Tractatus* Wittgenstein assumes, and does not try to stimulate, an interest in the kind of questions that Frege wrote about; he also takes it for granted that his readers will have read Frege.

Now, empiricist or idealist preconceptions, such as have been most common in philosophy for a long time, are a thorough impediment to the understanding of either Frege or the *Tractatus*. It is best, indeed, if one wants to understand these authors, not to have any philosophical preconceptions at all, but to be capable of being naively struck by such questions as the following ones: If I say that Russell is a clever philosopher, I mention Russell, and say something about him: now, is what I say about him something that I *mention*, just as I *mention* him? If so, what is the connection between these two mentioned things? If not, what account are we to give of the words expressing what I say about him? have they any reference to reality? Further, suppose we try to explain the reference to reality by adverting to the *truth* of what is said, then what about false statements? These *say that* such and such is the case just as much as true statements do—so that the *saying-that* done by true statements cannot be explained by their truth. The investigations prompted by these questions are more akin to ancient, than to more modern, philosophy.[1]

Again, if I say that the evening star is the same as the morning star, is this statement about the object mentioned, or about the signs used in speaking of it? If it is about the object, then why is it informative to say this, but not informative to say that the evening star is the same as the evening star? If it is about the signs, then, once more, how can it be informative since we can make signs stand for what we like by arbitrary definition?

This latter problem led Frege to formulate his famous distinction between the *sense* (*Sinn*) and the *reference* (*Bedeutung*) of words: The expressions 'the morning star' and 'the evening star', he said, have the same reference—for they refer to the same object, namely the planet Venus. But they have different senses, and that is why the statement of identity can be informative. This distinction between 'sense' and 'reference', once formulated, was used by Frege throughout his accounts of truth and falsehood, of objects and concepts, of propositions and thoughts.

[1] cf. Plato's *Theaetetus* 189A: 'In judging, one judges something; in judging something, one judges something real; so in judging something unreal one judges nothing; but judging nothing, one is not judging at all.' Wittgenstein returned to the problem presented by this argument again and again throughout his life.

Above all, Frege's enquiries were in no way psychological; nor had he any interest in private mental contents. If people speak of the number 100, they may have quite different images: one may have a mental picture of the letter C, another of ten rows of ten dots, another of a collection of hens in a yard; and the same man may have different images at different times, or again one may have no image. None of this has the slightest bearing on what is meant when we speak of the number 100. Nor can the history of the race or of language, nor again the mental processes by which a man grasps that $10 \times 10 = 100$, be relevant to the question what it is that he grasps.

Russell, who discusses many of the same questions as Frege, differs from him by introducing the notion of immediate experience, and hence that of private mental contents, into his explanations of meaning and his theory of judgment. For Russell was thoroughly imbued with the traditions of British empiricism. Wittgenstein's admirers have generally been like Russell in this, and have assumed that Wittgenstein was too; therefore they have had assumptions about what is fundamental in philosphical analysis which were quite out of tune with the *Tractatus*.

We owe to Frege the notion of a 'truth-value' which is current at the present day. The truth-value of a proposition is its truth or falsehood as the case may be. Frege says: its truth-value is *the true* if it is true and *the false* if it is false. This term is now very familiar to any student of elementary logic, and may easily seem to be no more than a conveniently short expression by means of which circumlocution is avoided. In Frege, however, we find it arrived at through hard work on the theory of meaning and truth: work which also produced other allied and fruitful conceptions.

One of the most important of these is the profound comparison[1] between a predicate and the expression of an arithmetical function, e.g. '$(x)^2$'. The notion of what is termed a 'propositional function', e.g. 'x is bald', is directly based on this comparison: here we get a proposition if we replace the 'x' by a (real) proper name, just as from '$(x)^2$' we get an expression of definite value by replacing the 'x' by a definite number. This comparison is fundamental to all modern logic.

[1] *See* Chapter 7.

Frege also gave us the modern conception of 'quantification', which is so useful and in such general use in logic that we regard it as we regard the wheel, forgetting its inventor. Quantification essentially consists in reformulating 'Everything is heavy' as: 'For all x, x is heavy'; and 'Something is heavy' as: 'For some x, x is heavy' or 'There is an x such that x is heavy'. These are written in a symbolic notation.[1]

The general reader may wonder at first whether the interest of such a device is not purely technical. It is easy to bring out that this is not so; it is of great general interest in philosophy.

For example, this formulation supplies us with a perspicuous refutation of the celebrated Ontological Argument of Descartes: people have been generally agreed that, but not how, it is to be refuted. According to the Ontological Argument the notion of God involves that of existence, as that of a triangle involves the various properties of a triangle; therefore, God exists. Let us concede the premise. (There is even good ground for it in the fact that e.g. 'There used to be a God, but isn't any more' seems to conflict with the concept 'God'.) The premise should be stated as follows: Just as, *if* anything is a triangle, it has those properties, so *if* anything is God, it must possess eternal existence. This is fair; we must be permitted to take seriously the argument about triangles which Descartes relies on. But in the sense in which the conclusion 'God exists' is intended, it means that *there is* a God. And that by no means follows from the premise. For, quite generally, from: 'For all x, if ϕx, then ψx', we cannot infer: 'There is an x such that ϕx.' That is, interpreting 'ϕx' as 'x is God' and 'ψx' as 'x has eternal existence', we cannot infer '*There is* a God' from 'For all x, if x is God, x has eternal existence'. We can very well grant that and still ask 'But *is* there such a being?' We may well say: 'It belongs to the concept of a phoenix never to die, but eternally to renew its life in the flames'; but we cannot infer from the concept that there lives such a creature.

Again, the following fallacious piece of reasoning is found in Aristotle: 'All chains of means to ends[2] must terminate in a final end. This final end will be the supreme good.' The first statement is

[1] *See* Glossary and Chapter 11.
[2] i.e. every case of doing a in order that b in order that c. . . .

reasonable; the second assumes that the first has shewn that there is some one end, the same for all chains of means to ends, in which they all terminate: the fallacy is immediately avoided by writing:

For all x, if x is a chain of means to ends, there is a y such that y is a final end and x terminates in y,
which is quite different from:

There is a y such that y is a final end, and for all x, if x is a chain of means to ends, x terminates in y.
It is of general usefulness to be armed against all fallacies of this type.

Again, a possible limitation on the sense in which a man is free can be brought out by considering that:

At all times there is a possibility of my abstaining from smoking, is quite different from and unluckily does not imply:

There is a possibility of my abstaining from smoking at all times. The difference here is quite easily made out in ordinary language; but it is also easily missed. In symbolic notation it cannot be missed, for there is no ambiguous way of writing down what we are saying.

Thus this device of modern logic at least is an instrument for the clarification of thought which is of use to anyone who engages in reasoning. And without the development of this part of logic by Frege and Russell, it is inconceivable that Wittgenstein should have written the *Tractatus*.

Russell, studying the same range of topics as Frege, criticized and rejected one of Frege's (at first sight) most plausible devices: the distinction between the sense and the reference of phrases. At the same time he used the new way of representing 'all' and 'some' in analysing sentences containing definite descriptions (singular descriptions preceded by the definite article).[1] Frege had treated such descriptions as proper names which, while they always had a sense, might or might not have a reference. According to him sentences containing definite descriptions without reference were neither true nor false. This view is dependent on the validity of the distinction between sense and reference, not merely as he first introduced it in connection with identity, but in the very extended application that he made of it; if that has to be rejected, a new

[1] *See* Chapter 2.

account of such sentences has to be found. This was given by Russell in his Theory of Descriptions. Wittgenstein embraced the logical analysis afforded by Russell's theory with admiration, and, as we shall see, it exercised a great influence on the thought of the *Tractatus*.

The notions of 'sense', 'reference' and 'meaning' as they occur in these three authors, Frege, Russell and Wittgenstein, perhaps need a summary account. Frege's 'sense' corresponds roughly to the ordinary English 'meaning'. When we ask for the meaning of a phrase, we are not asking to have an object indicated to us: we want a paraphrase with the same meaning—or, as Frege would say, the same sense. On the other hand, if I say 'When I spoke of "that fat charlatan", I *meant* Smith', what I 'meant' is a man; Frege's 'reference' (*Bedeutung*) corresponds to what is 'meant' in this use of of the word.

Wittgenstein follows Frege in this use of the words '*Bedeutung*', '*bedeuten*'. Generally, in the *Tractatus*, they ought not to be rendered, as C. K. Ogden[1] rendered them, by 'meaning' and 'mean', but rather by 'reference' and 'stand for'. Wittgenstein's conception of 'sense' may be called the same as Frege's, if we are careful to add that Wittgenstein had different *theses* about it: for he held that names had no sense but only reference, and propositions no reference but only sense; and also that a proposition could not have a sense without being either true or false. Further, he uses the suggestion of 'direction' that is contained in the word 'sense' when he speaks of positive and negative as opposite senses: we shall see that he considered significant negatability to be of the essence of a significant proposition, and a proposition and its negation as like arrows pointing in opposite directions. ('*Sinn*' is ordinary German for 'direction'; in English usage 'sense' occurs with that meaning in mathematics.)

Russell uses only one notion 'meaning' and holds that the meanings of words must always be objects that one is directly

[1] English readers of the *Tractatus* may need to be warned that Ogden's translation is notoriously very bad. Wittgenstein told me that he had not checked the whole of this translation, but only answered a few questions that were put to him about some passages. e.g. I think we can see Wittgenstein's hand in the free but excellent rendering of 4.023.

acquainted with. He also speaks of 'denoting': a 'denoting' expression is such an expression as 'Some ambassador', 'Any horse', 'The (one and only) earth satellite'. It was the object of the Theory of Descriptions to analyse such expressions away, and so 'denoting' has no part in Russell's final explanation.

This, then, is the historical background of the *Tractatus*. It is a book which is apt to captivate people's minds, while at the same time seeming in many parts excessively obscure. Some people, once they have looked into it, are prevented from throwing it away in despair of penetrating its meaning by the impression they receive of great light in certain areas. This *Introduction* is addressed primarily to such readers as these. It is certainly not meant to be of any value to someone who does not read or propose to read the *Tractatus* itself.

The *Tractatus* is not presented in an order of demonstration from premises; if we want to find the grounds for its contentions, we must look in the middle and not at the beginning. It is divided into a set of numbered remarks in a decimal notation shewing what is of greater and what of subsidiary importance: the more decimal places in a number, the more subsidiary the remark it is attached to. The main propositions are the ones numbered with the whole numbers 1—7. These run:

1. The world is everything that is the case.
2. What is the case—the fact—is the existence of atomic facts.[1]
3. The logical picture[2] of the facts is the thought.
4. The thought is the significant proposition.
5. The proposition is a truth-function[3] of elementary propositions.[4]
   (The elementary proposition is a truth-function of itself.)
6. The general form of truth-function is $[\bar{p}, \bar{\xi}, N(\bar{\xi})]$.[5] This is the general form of proposition.
7. What we cannot speak of, we must be silent about.[6]

[1] *See* Chapters 1 and 4.
[2] *See* Chapter 4.
[3] *See* Glossary and Chapter 3.
[4] *See* Chapter 1.
[5] *See* Chapter 10.
[6] *See* Chapters 5 and 13.

It is clear enough from this that the principal theme of the book is the connection between language, or thought, and reality. The main thesis about this is that sentences, or their mental counterparts, are pictures of facts. Only we must not suppose that what is pictured by a proposition has to exist: as Wittgenstein wrote in explaining himself to Russell in 1919, a fact is what corresponds to a proposition *if* it is true. The proposition is the same picture whether it is true or false—i.e. whether the fact it is a picture of *is* a fact, is the case, or not. This should not make us ask 'How, then, can a fact not be a fact?' For, following Wittgenstein's explanation, it means: The proposition is the same picture whether what corresponds to it *if* it is true is the case or not: it is a picture of that. And what corresponds to it if it is true is the same, whether it is true or false. The world is the totality of facts—i.e. of the counterparts in reality of *true* propositions. And nothing but picturable situations can be stated in propositions. There is indeed much that is inexpressible—which we must not try to state, but must contemplate without words.

In his Introduction Wittgenstein suggests that he may be understood only by people who have had the same thoughts as he; certainly he can only be understood by people who have been perplexed by the same problems. His own writing is extraordinarily compressed, and it is necessary to ponder each word in order to understand his sentences. When one does this, they often turn out to be quite straightforward, and by no means so oracular or aphoristic as they have been taken to be. But few authors make such demands on the close attention and active co-operation of their readers.

In my account, I have not followed the arrangement of the *Tractatus* at all. That, I think, is something to do when one reads the book for enjoyment *after* one has come to understand its main ideas. I have chosen what seem to me to be the most important themes and problems of the book. My first six chapters aim at giving the reader some idea of the 'picture theory' of the proposition. I devote a great deal of space to the topic of negation, for 'not', which is so simple to use, is utterly mystifying to think about; no theory of thought or judgment which does not give an account of it can hope to be adequate. It is thus one of the central topics of the *Tractatus*.

Chapter 7 is mainly concerned with what becomes of the great problem of Universals in Wittgenstein's theory, and Chapter 8 with certain aspects of 'not', 'and', 'or', etc., which are not covered in my account of the picture theory. Chapters 9 and 10 deal with important technical notions which are rather special to the *Tractatus*, and could be omitted by a beginner who wanted first to familiarize himself with its foundations: these chapters, we may say, treat of the upper storeys of the edifice. But with Chapter 11, on the theory of generality, we are once more working on the foundations. The last two chapters are about some general philosophical consequences which Wittgenstein drew from his investigations into the philosophy of logic.

The logic, a knowledge of which is necessary for an understanding of the *Tractatus*, is very elementary; my own aim has been to write in such a way that someone who was not already familiar with it could pick it up as he went along. In case the symbols and technical terms of elementary modern logic should be unfamiliar to a reader, I append a short glossary.

GLOSSARY

p, q, r	These small letters are used to represent propositions. (By Wittgenstein, only for elementary propositions.)
a, b, c	These small letters (from the beginning of the alphabet) are used to represent proper names of objects.
fa, ga, ϕa, ψa	represent propositions containing the name 'a'. Similarly
f(a,b), ϕ(a,b)	represent a proposition containing the names 'a' and 'b': 'f' and 'ϕ' are here shewn to be 'two-place' predicates, or 'dyadic relational expressions'.
R, S	These large letters are used to represent relations, e.g. 'to the right of', 'larger than', 'father of'. And
aRb	symbolizes a proposition asserting a relation between a and b.
x, y, z	These small letters (from the end of the alphabet) mark (different) empty places in propositions written in the forms 'fa' or 'f(a,b)', or 'aRb', from which a proper name or names have been removed; e.g. if we remove 'a' and 'b' from 'aRb' we have '–R–', which yields a proposition if we put names in the blanks. To differentiate blanks, we put 'xRy'; to shew they are to be filled up the same way, we put 'xRx'.

Variable	Such a small letter as x, y, z, in the role just described. Variables are chiefly used in the construction of
Quantified propositions	Propositions containing the notions 'all', 'some'. When we are speaking of 'all' so-and-so, and any example of so-and-so would be an object which could have a proper name, the proposition is written in the form:
$(x)\phi x$	For all x, ϕx; i.e. 'Everything is ϕ'.
$(Ex)\phi x$	For some x, ϕx; i.e. 'Something is ϕ' or 'There is an x such that ϕx'.
Truth-value	The truth or falsehood (as the case may be) of a proposition.
Function (Value, Argument)	Cannot be defined, but only illustrated: a *function*, say $(\ )^2$, takes different *values* for different *arguments*: e.g. the value of the function $(\ )^2$ for the argument 3 is 9, since $(3)^2=9$. The value of the power function $(\ )^{(\ )}$ for arguments 2 and 3 in that order is 8: since 2 to the power 3 (2^3) is 8.
Truth-function	A function (e.g. '– and –') whose argument(s) (e.g. 'p' and 'q') and values (e.g. 'p and q') are propositions, such that the truth-value of its value is determined by the truth-value(s) of its argument(s).
Truth-functional connectives (one kind of 'logical constants')	Signs used to express truth-functions, e.g. 'not', 'and', 'or'. For the truth-value of 'not-p' is determined by the truth-value of p, and the truth-value of 'p and q' and 'p or q' is determined by the truth-values of p and of q.

∼ not.

. and.

∨ or; non-exclusive, i.e. ‘p ∨ q’ is true when both ‘p’ and ‘q’ are true, as well as when only one of them is.

⊃ if . . . then . . . , defined as ‘either not . . . or . . .’. Thus ‘p⊃q’ is true if ‘p’ is false or ‘q’ true, regardless of any real connection in their subject-matters. This (minimum) sense of ‘if . . . then’ occurs in ‘If that is so, I’m a Dutchman’, which if I am known not to be a Dutchman is a way of saying that ‘that’ is *not* so.

Material implication the ‘if . . . then’ expressed by ‘⊃’.

Truth-table[1] (or: Matrix) A table designed to show the relation between the truth-value of a truth-function and the truth-value(s) of its argument(s). Thus the truth-tables for ‘p and q’ and ‘p or q’ are:

p	q	p and q	p or q
T(rue)	T	T	T
T	F	F	T
F(alse)	T	F	T
F	F	F	F

Tautology Any truth-function such that whatever the truth-values of its arguments, its value for those arguments is always true. Examples: p ∨ ∼p; (p.p⊃q)⊃q.

Logical product Conjunction of all the propositions of a given set, e.g. p. q. r.

Logical sum Disjunction of all the propositions of a given set, e.g. p ∨ q ∨ r.

[1] Invented (independently) by Wittgenstein and Post.

$=$	In logical contexts this is used as the sign of identity, not of equality in quantity; 'a=b' means that a *is* b.
N( )	Joint negation of the propositions put between the brackets; used only by Wittgenstein (*see* Chapter 10).
O, Ω	variable signs for an operation in Wittgenstein's sense; these symbols are peculiar to the *Tractatus* (*see* Chapter 9).
ξ, η	variables for expressions, not tied to any one kind, as is x, which is a name variable, or again n, which is a numerical variable: used in informal exposition by Frege and Wittgenstein.
ר	sign for a special operation, used only in the present book (*see* Chapter 10). Read as 'Resh'.

1

ELEMENTARY PROPOSITIONS

Karl Popper has described the *Tractatus* in the following way:

> 'Wittgenstein tried to shew that all so-called philosophical or metaphysical propositions were in fact non-propositions or pseudo-propositions: that they were senseless or meaningless. All genuine (or meaningful) propositions were truth-functions of the elementary or atomic propositions which described "atomic facts", i.e. facts which can in principle be ascertained by observation. In other words, they were fully reducible to elementary or atomic propositions which were simple statements describing possible states of affairs, and which could be in principle established or rejected by observation. If we call a statement an "observation statement" not only if it states an actual observation but also if it states anything that may be observed, we shall have to say that every genuine proposition must be a truth-function of and therefore deducible from, observation statements. All other apparent propositions will be, in fact, nonsense; they will be meaningless pseudo-propositions.'[1]

I cite this passage because it expresses the most common view of the *Tractatus*. It only needs a small supplement to express that view completely. For it is sufficiently well known that the *Tractatus* contains a 'picture theory' of language, of which Popper here makes no mention. The whole theory of propositions is, then, on this view, a merely external combination of two theories: a 'picture theory' of elementary propositions (viz. that they have meaning by being

[1] *British Philosophy in Mid-Century*, Allen and Unwin, 1957: pp. 163–4.

'logical pictures' of elementary states of affairs), and the theory of truth-functions as an account of non-elementary propositions; this latter theory breaks down rather easily, because it is impossible to regard generalized propositions that relate to an infinitely numerous universe as truth-functions of elementary propositions.

Someone who, having read the *Tractatus*, reads Popper's account of it, must be struck by one thing: namely that there is a great deal about 'observation' in Popper's account, and very little about it in the *Tractatus*. According to Popper, the elementary propositions of the *Tractatus* are simple observation statements. Now can we find any support for this view in the *Tractatus* itself? I think that the strongest support that we can find is at 3.263: 'The references of primitive signs can be made clear by elucidations. Elucidations are propositions containing the primitive signs. Thus they can only be understood, if one is acquainted with the references of these signs.' I think we can take it that 'primitive signs' are the same thing as 'names', from the passage above, 3.261: 'Two signs, one a primitive sign, and the other defined by means of primitive signs, cannot signify in the same way. *Names* cannot be expounded by means of definitions.' Here it is clear enough that 'names' are 'primitive signs'; and as we know from elsewhere that Wittgenstein did not regard logical signs as primitive signs, or as having anything that they stand for, we can also say that the only primitive signs for him are what he calls 'names'. Names, then, can be made clear by elucidations, by sentences containing them spoken to someone who is acquainted with the objects that they stand for.

An obvious example of a name might seem to be the word 'red' uttered in a sentence, perhaps 'Red patch here' in the presence of someone who is contemplating the red patch and who may be supposed to have acquaintance with the object designated by the word 'red'. And 'red patch here' would seem to be a candidate for being a simple or elementary observation statement such as Popper refers to. This suggests that the elementary propositions are not merely observation statements, but sense-datum statements; as, indeed, they were taken to be both by many members of the Vienna Circle and for many years in Cambridge discussions. And I think it is quite possible that Wittgenstein had roughly this sort of thing rather vaguely in mind. His speaking of 'acquaintance' (for that certainly seems the best rendering of '*kennen*' and its compounds where they occur in the *Tractatus*) very strongly suggests this; we immediately think of Russell's distinction between 'knowledge by acquaintance' and 'knowledge by description'.

I do not believe that any other support for Popper's view of elementary propositions is to be found in the *Tractatus*. And this passage is a rather slender support.

In the first place, Wittgenstein does not state, or even suggest, that the proposition which contains an elementary name and 'elucidates' that name for a person acquainted with its reference must be an elementary proposition.

In the second place, the kind of example that comes most readily to mind, 'This is a red patch', can be proved not to be an elementary proposition according to the *Tractatus*. For at 6.3751 we find in parenthesis: 'It is clear that the logical product of two elementary propositions can be neither a tautology nor a contradiction. The assertion that a point in the visual field is two different colours at the same time is a contradiction.' It follows directly from this that 'This is a red patch' cannot be an elementary proposition.

Indeed, quite generally, if elementary propositions are simple observation statements, it is very difficult to see how what Wittgenstein says here can possibly hold good of them; for, for any proposition which could reasonably be called a 'simple observation statement', one could find another that would be incompatible with it and be precisely analogous to it logically. Therefore, whatever elementary propositions may be, they are not simple observation statements; and this accounts for the lack of reference to observation in all the remarks concerning elementary propositions; which would surely be very strange if Popper's interpretation were the correct one.

With this is connected the fact that there is hardly any epistemology in the *Tractatus*; and that Wittgenstein evidently did not think that epistemology had any bearing on his subject-matter. We find epistemology put in its place at 4.1121: 'Psychology is no nearer related to philosophy than is any other natural science. The theory of knowledge is the philosophy of psychology.'

A letter to Russell in 1919, written from the prison camp at Monte

Cassino, throws further light on this. Russell had asked: '. . . But a *Gedanke* [thought] is a *Tatsache* [fact]: what are its constituents and components, and what is their relation to those of the pictured *Tatsache*?' To this Wittgenstein replies: 'I don't know *what* the constituents of a thought are but I know *that* it must have constituents which correspond to the words of language. Again the kind of relation of the constituents of the thought and of the pictured fact is irrelevant. It would be a matter of psychology to find out.' That is to say, it would be a matter of empirical investigation to find out, both what the constituents of a thought are and how they are related to the 'objects' occurring in facts, that is to say, to the objects designated by the 'names' in language.

That this is fantastically untrue is shewn by any serious investigation into epistemology, such as Wittgenstein made in *Philosophical Investigations*. But it is fair to say that at the time when he wrote the *Tractatus*, Wittgenstein pretended that epistemology had nothing to do with the foundations of logic and the theory of meaning, with which he was concerned. The passage about the 'elucidation' of names, where he says that one must be 'acquainted' with their objects, gives him the lie.

More positively, the grounds on which Wittgenstein holds that there are elementary propositions and simple names shew that the elementary propositions have not the role of simple observation statements. At 5.5562 we find: 'If we know, on purely logical grounds, that there must be elementary propositions, then this must be known by anyone who understands propositions in their unanalysed form.' But it is clear that he thought we did know this on purely logical grounds. That is to say, the character of inference, and of meaning itself, *demands* that there should be elementary propositions. And that there should be simple names and simple objects is equally presented as a *demand* at 3.23: 'The demand for the possibility of the simple signs is the demand for definiteness of sense.' We shall see that he holds that an indefinite sense would not be a sense at all; indeed in the Preface he put this forward, not just as one of the most important contentions of the book, but as an epitome of its whole meaning: 'Whatever can be said at all, can be said clearly; and what we cannot speak of, we must be silent on.'

Again, the simple objects are presented as something demanded by the nature of language at 2.021, 2.0211: 'The objects form the substance of the world. That is why they cannot be complex. If the world had no substance, then one proposition's making sense would depend on another one's being true.' But this is not the case: we can *devise* propositions at will and know what they mean, without ascertaining any facts. If one proposition's making sense always depended on another one's being true, then it would be impossible to do this—impossible, as Wittgenstein puts it, to *devise* a picture of the world (true or false) (2.0212); he means by this no more than devising a proposition.

We get further (though, I should judge, unnecessary) confirmation from an entry in the notebooks out of which he composed the *Tractatus*, in which he remarks (23.5.15): 'It also seems certain that we do not infer the existence of simple objects from the existence of particular simple objects, but rather know them—by description, as it were—as the end product of analysis, by means of a process leading to them.' The thought of this entry in the notebooks is in fact echoed in the *Tractatus* text at 4.221: 'It is obvious that in analysing propositions we must arrive at elementary propositions consisting of names in immediate combination.' This view of names, and hence of our knowledge of objects, is a more truthful one than is suggested by the remark about 'elucidations'. And in the notebooks he exclaims at the fact that he is absolutely certain that there are elementary propositions, atomic facts, and simple objects, even though he cannot produce one single example.

If the elementary propositions of the *Tractatus* are not simple observation statements, it seems necessary to find some other account of them before we can grasp the doctrines of the book even in vague outline. For an understanding of the notion of an elementary proposition will help us with its correlate, an atomic fact, or elementary situation.

Wittgenstein opens the *Tractatus* by saying that the world is the totality of facts (*Tatsachen*). He quickly introduces a new term (translated 'atomic fact'): '*Sachverhalt*'. Literally this word simply means 'situation'. Etymologically it suggests 'hold of things'—i.e. a way things stand in relation to one another. Wittgenstein plays heavily on this suggestion. It rapidly becomes clear that by a 'situation' he means an arrangement of objects, which objects, he says, are 'simple'. The 'situation' is a concatenation of simple objects, which 'hang in one another like the links of a chain' (2.03). Hence the word was translated 'atomic fact'; for 'situation', not carrying with it the special suggestion of '*Sachverhalt*', would have been obscure; and 'atomic fact' had been Russell's term for the correlate of a true 'atomic' proposition.

Writing to Russell from Monte Cassino in 1919, Wittgenstein explained *Sachverhalt* as what corresponds to an elementary proposition if it is true, and a *Tatsache* as what corresponds to the logical product (i.e. the conjunction) of elementary propositions when this product is true.[1] This explanation concerns the first introduction of '*Tatsache*' or 'fact'. At 2.06 he introduced the further expression 'a negative fact': 'We also call the non-existence of atomic facts a negative fact.'

That is to say, to the question 'What is a fact?' we must answer: 'It is nothing but the existence of atomic facts.' This is a thesis about facts; not the assignment of a technical meaning to the word in Wittgenstein's system. And to the question: 'Is there such a thing as a negative fact?' we must answer: 'That is only the non-existence of atomic facts.' Thus the notion of a fact is supposed to be explained to us by means of that of an atomic fact, or elementary situation. And that in turn is simply what corresponds to a true elementary proposition. Thus an exploration of this notion is indispensable.

[1] Some critics have objected to the translation 'atomic fact' because an atomic fact is presumably a fact, and it is awkward to speak of 'non-existent facts'; but Wittgenstein does speak of non-existent *Sachverhalte* (2.06). This objection does not amount to much. But it is added that Wittgenstein never speaks of 'possible facts' (*Tatsachen*). For what he speaks of as possible, he uses another German word, *Sachlage*, which means 'state of affairs'. Prof. Stenius suggests that this is the real non-atomic parallel to *Sachverhalt*, and that Wittgenstein was simply wrong in giving Russell parallel accounts of *Sachverhalt* and *Tatsache*. I find suggestions that Wittgenstein gave an incorrect account of the *Tractatus* in 1919 quite unacceptable. In German a 'possible fact' (*mögliche Tatsache*) would be something that is *perhaps* a fact—i.e. for all we know to the contrary; this irrelevant reference to our knowledge would surely be what ruled the phrase out. The difficulties we encounter here are really those of the subject-matter itself, and not of Wittgenstein's terminology. Wittgenstein accepted the translation 'atomic fact'.

The following appear to be theses which hold for elementary propositions:

(1) They are a class of mutually independent propositions.
(2) They are essentially positive.
(3) They are such that for each of them there are no two ways of being true or false, but only one.
(4) They are such that there is in them no distinction between an internal and an external negation.
(5) They are concatenations of names, which are absolutely simple signs.

As for the reasons for holding that there are such propositions as these, we know at least that, according to the *Tractatus*, they are 'purely logical'. About these purely logical grounds I will only say here that the main one is this: we can draw conclusions from a false proposition. This is the same fact as that we can invent or devise a proposition and know what it means, without first discovering the facts which hold in regard to its subject-matter. For to understand a proposition is to know what is the case *if* it is true.

The five theses which hold good of elementary propositions can be found at or inferred from several places in the *Tractatus*.

(1) *Elementary propositions are a class of mutually independent propositions*. This we have already seen stated in a restricted form at 6.3751: 'It is clear that the logical product of two elementary propositions can neither be a tautology nor a contradiction.'[1] Strictly, it may be said that this might be true and the general mutual independence false; but we need not delay over the suggestion. It is worth noticing that the existence of a great class of mutually independent propositions is implicit in the common explanation of truth-functions and truth-functional tautologies. For we are told that a complex proposition is a truth-function of the proposition(s) contained in it if its truth-value is uniquely determined by the truth-value of the proposition(s) in question; and it is a tautology if it is true for all combinations of the truth-values of its components. If it is a function of several propositions, it is impossible that its tautological truth should consist in its truth for all the combinations unless its components have

[1] And also 4.211 and 5.134.

some mutual independence. To take an example, the syllogism 'If all Europeans are white and some Europeans are Mohammedans, then some white men are Mohammedans' is a logical truth in which three propositions occur; its being a logical truth is equivalent to the logical impossibility of the case in which the first two component propositions are true and the last false. A truth-table will thus not display the tautological character of the proposition; for if one constructs a truth-table for 'If p and q, then r', one has to show the truth-value (namely falsehood) of this conditional for the case where 'p' and 'q' are both true but 'r' is false; and it is not the truth-table but the interpretation of 'p', 'q', and 'r' which shows that in the syllogistic case the conditional cannot be false.

Nevertheless a truth-table containing inconsistent rows *may* display the tautological character of a proposition. e.g. Aristotle felt a difficulty about the following form of geometrical argument: 'All triangles are either isosceles[1] or scalene; all isosceles triangles have the property ϕ; all scalene triangles have the property ϕ; therefore all triangles have the property ϕ.' We can see that his difficulty consisted in the argument's not being formalizable in his syllogistic calculus. What he needed was the truth-functional calculus. Let x be a figure; then let 'p'='x is a triangle', 'q'='x is isosceles', 'r'='x is scalene', and 's'='x has the property ϕ'. Then the fact that $(p \supset q \vee r.\ q \supset s.\ r \supset s) \supset (p \supset s)$[2] is a tautology of the truth-functional calculus would have supplied the missing formalization. Now being a tautology means being true for all combinations of the possible truth-values of the elements (means being, as logicians say, a tautology *of* the given elements), and the truth-table setting forth these combinations will include a row in which both 'q' and 'r' are true, and another in which both 'q' and 'r' are false while 'p' is true. But if 'q'='x is isosceles', and 'r'='x is scalene', these combinations will be impossible.

We may conclude from this that a complex proposition can be shewn to be a logical truth from the fact that it is a tautology of its component propositions, even though some of these are mutually

[1] i.e. possessed of at least two equal sides.

[2] In English 'p implies that q or r, and q implies that s, and r implies that s, all implies that p implies that s'.

inconsistent; and from the syllogistic example, that it cannot be shewn *not* to be a logical truth from the fact that it is *not* a tautology of its component propositions.[1] Nevertheless, the type of tautology in which some of the combinations of truth-possibilities are inconsistent must be regarded as degenerate. The fact that by our calculus the complex proposition turns out 'true' if we assign an inconsistent set of truth-values to its components does not help to demonstrate its tautological character; we might rather strike out inconsistent rows of the truth-table as not counting. But if all cases were like this, with now one now another row of our truth-tables inconsistent, then the *formal* truth of the truth-functional tautology would vanish.

Thus either the theory of truth-functions has no application, or there is a class of mutually independent propositions. But we apply the calculus of truth-functions every time we reason e.g. 'If p, then q, but not q, therefore not p': a thing which we constantly do in the most diverse contexts of ordinary life. Here is the beginning of a justification for Wittgenstein's saying: 'We know on purely logical grounds that there must be elementary propositions' and 'everyone knows this who understands propositions in their unanalysed form'. At any rate everyone manifests an implicit knowledge that there is a (very large) class of mutually independent propositions.

(2) *Elementary propositions are essentially positive.* This we can infer from 4.25: 'If the elementary proposition is true, the atomic fact exists; if it is false the atomic fact does not exist' together with 2.06: 'We also call the existence of atomic facts a positive, and their non-existence a negative fact': the elementary proposition therefore is such as to express something *positive*, namely the holding of an elementary situation. This, of course, does not mean that the occurrence of the sign of negation in a propositional sign would prove that it did not state an elementary proposition. Wittgenstein warns us at 4.0621: 'The occurrence of negation in a proposition is

[1] According to Wittgenstein, this logical truth can be exhibited as a tautology of a set of elementary propositions, though not as a tautology of the propositions explicitly occurring in it; *see* Chapter 11. Von Wright has shown a simple way of exhibiting it as a tautology if we assume men to have any given finite number; *see Logical Studies* (Routledge & Kegan Paul, 1957), Chapter I; it is exhibited as a tautology of singular propositions about men.

not *enough* to characterize its sense'—i.e. to characterize it as negative rather than positive in sense; as stating, if true, a negative fact.

Russell in his letters to Wittgenstein after receiving the text of the *Tractatus* once asked whether the negations of elementary propositions were themselves elementary propositions, and received the indignant-sounding rejoinder: 'Of course not.'

(3) *Elementary propositions are such that for them there are no two ways of being true or false but only one.*

This is clearest for falsehood. By 4.25 the falsehood of an elementary proposition is simply the non-existence of a single atomic situation.

At 3.24 Wittgenstein says: 'A complex can be given only by its description, which will hold or not hold. The proposition in which there is mention of a complex will not be meaningless when the complex does not exist, but merely false. That a propositional element designates a complex can be seen from an indefiniteness in the propositions in which it occurs.' One kind of indefiniteness in a proposition might be that there was more than one way of its being false: the complex might exist, but what was said of it might not hold; or the complex might not exist.

We could imagine a proposition in which there was mention of a complex, which had only one way of being true, though two ways of being false. Let us suppose a proposition 'ϕa' such that 'a' is a simple name, ϕ being such that there was only one way for ϕ to hold of anything. Then let us suppose a complex A, which exists if bRc. Then 'ϕA' will be false if A exists but ϕ does not hold of it, and also if not bRc, so there are two ways for it to be false; but only one way for it to be true, namely that bRc, so that A exists, and ϕA.

'We *know*,' Wittgenstein goes on, 'that not everything is settled by such a proposition'—that is to say, by a proposition in which there is mention of a complex. In the example that I have imagined, 'everything would be settled' by the *truth* of the proposition, but not everything by its falsehood. What he principally had in mind was the sort of proposition where there is a variety of ways for the proposition to be true. (This is in fact the most ordinary sort of proposition, of which alone one can give examples; to illustrate other sorts of proposition one has to use dummy names and dummy predicates and stipulate their characters.) Take for example 'My watch is lying on the table', which Wittgenstein considers in his notebooks. There are hundreds of different, more minutely statable, and incompatible states of affairs which would make that proposition true. The elementary proposition will have only one state of affairs that will make it true: 'everything' will be settled by it—i.e. nothing be left open.

(4) *Elementary propositions are such that there is in them no distinction between an internal and an external negation.* This is in part the same point as has already been made in connection with definiteness of sense. We can say: 'The King of France is bald' has as *a* negation 'The King of France is not bald'; I distinguish this *internal* negation of the proposition from the *external* negation: 'Not: The King of France is bald'—we have already seen how these differ in sense. To take another case: the proposition 'Everyone is wise' has an *internal* negation, 'Everyone is not wise' (or: 'is unwise'), and another, *external*, negation: 'Not everyone is wise.' Aristotle was rather puzzled by this difference between 'Socrates is wise' and 'Everyone is wise': if 'Socrates is wise' is untrue, then 'Socrates is not wise' is true; but if 'Everyone is wise' is untrue, still it does not follow that 'Everyone is not wise', or 'is unwise', is true; the contradictory is the different proposition that not everyone is wise.

It is true that we sometimes use 'Everyone is not . . .' in the sense 'Not everyone is . . .'; and hence it is convenient to use the term 'unwise' to make our point. But, to adapt what Frege says,[1] it should not be supposed from this attachment of the negation to 'wise' that 'what is negated is the content, not of the whole sentence, but just of this part. . . . It is incorrect to say: "Because the negative syllable is combined with part of the sentence, the sense of the whole sentence is not negated." On the contrary; it is by combining the negative syllable with a part of the sentence that we do negate . . . the whole sentence.' That is to say, the sentence 'Everyone is wise' is certainly made out to be untrue by someone who says 'Everyone is unwise'; but this is still a different negation from that expressed by 'Not everyone is wise'.

[1] Negation, *Philosophical Writings of Gottlob Frege*, ed. Geach & Black (Blackwell, 1952), p. 131.

I choose 'internal' and 'external' merely as convenient labels to attach to these negations. An elementary proposition will be one for which no such difference, between an internal and an external negation, can be found. The falsehood of the elementary proposition never consists in anything but the non-existence of a single atomic fact.

(5) *Elementary propositions are concatenations of names.* This we find stated explicitly at 4.22: 'The elementary proposition consists of names. It is a connection, a concatenation, of names.' Names are simple signs; this is not merely asserted, but argued for, in the *Tractatus*, at 3.3411: 'So it could be said that the real name is what all symbols that designate the object have in common. Then we could get the result, in a number of steps, that no kind of composition was essential to the name.' That is to say, any name will of course have a certain physical complexity, but you could replace it by another, with a different complexity, without detriment to its doing the job of naming the object. Whereas you could not, for example, adequately symbolize a relation without using a symbol whose complexity enabled you to shew the difference between, say, aRb and bRa.

So far what is argued about names would seem to be perfectly applicable to ordinary names, such as 'Wittgenstein', which are not names in the sense of the *Tractatus*. 'Wittgenstein' is what he calls a 'simple symbol' at 3.24: 'The contraction of the symbol of a complex into a simple symbol can be expressed by means of a definition.' This 'definition' will be basically the same thing as the 'description' which he speaks of as 'giving' the complex.

Now the physical complexity of the name 'Wittgenstein' expresses nothing, as can be shewn in the way suggested. But if the 'real' name, or 'real' symbol, of the object called Wittgenstein, has something about it that implies complexity, then the name can be said not to be a logically simple sign, even though it appears as a simple sign in the sentence. For, as it is put at 3.262: 'What does not get expressed in the signs is shewn by their application. Their application declares what the signs fail to bring out.' And the application of the name 'Wittgenstein' brings out that a great many things, and a great variety of things, have to be true in order for there to be true statements in which the name occurs. The same would be true of any sign which had the same function as this sign 'Wittgenstein'. But what is common to all the symbols with this function is what is essential to the symbol, as has been said at 3.341: 'In general what is essential about a symbol is what all symbols capable of fulfilling the same function have in common.' Therefore a certain complexity, which only comes out in the application, is essential to the name 'Wittgenstein'.

Thus the true names of the *Tractatus* will be, not physically simple signs, but ones lacking the sort of complexity that the name 'Wittgenstein' has; and it is clear that elementary propositions can contain only such names, since if they contained names like 'Wittgenstein' they could not have only one way of being true or false.

So much here for the simplicity of names; we must now discuss 'concatenation'. The metaphor of a chain should suggest an essential feature of elementary propositions. As we have seen, what is expressed by calling an elementary proposition a concatenation is expressed for elementary situations ('atomic facts') at 2.03: 'In the atomic fact the objects hang in one another like the links of a chain.' In a literal chain consisting of links

A—B—C—D

there is no difference between A's being linked to the B end of the chain B—C—D, and D's being linked to the C end of the chain A—B—C. I think this element in the analogy should be taken seriously; in the elementary proposition there must be nothing corresponding to bracketing.

Let us look at what Wittgenstein says about bracketing at 5.461–5.4611: 'The apparently unimportant fact that logical pseudo-relations like ∨ (or) and ⊃ (if . . ., then . . .)—as opposed to real relations—require brackets is significant.' This remark has been criticized on the ground that a bracketless notation, such as that invented by Łukasiewicz, is possible. In this notation we write

Cpq

instead of

p⊃q

and then the difference between

$$(p\supset q)\supset r$$

and

$$p\supset(q\supset r)$$

will be expressed by the difference between

$$C(Cpq)r$$

and

$$Cp(Cqr)$$

where, though I have put brackets in, these are only an aid to reading and are not needed to resolve any ambiguity. Now this is of course true; it is true because the collecting done by brackets is done by the rule for reading an expression containing 'C'. Some method of collecting is required, and that is the essential point. 'Logical operation signs are punctuation marks,' Wittgenstein says, and Łukasiewicz's notation, far from refuting Wittgenstein's remarks about brackets, brings out what Wittgenstein meant, for in it the collecting or punctuating normally done by brackets is done by the rule for reading the logical operation-signs. Now if the chain metaphor is to be taken seriously, this differentiation of meanings by punctuation or collection must somehow be inapplicable to the elementary proposition.

What I call 'collection' or 'punctuation' can occur in propositions other than those (overtly) containing truth-functional connectives. Consider the sentence 'Every man loves some girl.' We may regard this as splitting up into three 'expressions': 'Every man', 'loves' and 'some girl'. It is useful here to adopt the metaphor of structural formulae in chemistry for the structure of sentences. An expression will then sometimes correspond to what chemists call a 'radical': that is, a group of atoms which cannot by itself form a stable molecule, but which can in chemical transformations pass from one compound into another without the break-up of its own inner connection of atoms. And the fact that what compound you have depends, not only on what radicals you have, but also on how they are fitted together, would be a parallel to such a difference as that between 'Socrates loves Plato' and 'Plato loves Socrates', or again 'Every man loves some girl' and 'Some girl loves every man'. There is, however, a difference between two possible senses of 'Every man loves some girl' which *could* be brought out by a difference of bracketing. In

(Every man) (loves some girl)

we could take the bracketing as indicating that 'every man' is supplied as an argument in

—loves some girl

and the sense will be that the predicate 'loves some girl' is true of every man; whereas in

(Every man loves) (some girl)

'some girl' is supplied as an argument in

Every man loves—

and the sense will be that of some girl it is true that every man loves her. The difference is of course the one usually brought out by the order of quantifiers.[1] This difference is one that cannot be illustrated by our chemical analogy. And it is a sort of possibility of difference that has to be absent from the elementary proposition.

Contrast with this case 'Socrates loves Plato'. We can indeed introduce two different bracketings: '(Socrates) (loves Plato)', which asserts of Socrates that he loves Plato, and '(Socrates loves) (Plato)', which asserts of Plato that Socrates loves him. But in this case Wittgenstein, following Frege, would say that there was absolutely no difference of sense.

Now it seems plausible to say that the reason why we have an ambiguity resoluble by brackets in the one case but not in the other

[1] *See* Chapter 11, pp. 138-41.

is that, at any rate as compared with 'Every man' and 'some girl', the *expressions* 'Socrates' and 'Plato' are simple. This sort of consideration may lead us to divine behind our propositions a kind of proposition to which the chemical analogy of radicals will apply perfectly; unlike a proposition in which, though you have the same expressions combined in the same way, it makes a difference by what stages you conceive the proposition as built up. Such a proposition will be a concatenation of really simple signs, which have indeed an accidental complexity, but one irrelevant to their function as signs.

2

THE THEORY OF DESCRIPTIONS

Wittgenstein's 'picture theory' of the proposition is much influenced by Russell's Theory of Descriptions. According to that theory, definite descriptions such as 'the author of Waverley', and 'the present King of France', and again indefinite descriptions like 'a man' as this phrase occurs in 'I met a man', or 'A man has been here', are not the designating expressions they at first seem to be.

At first sight, one readily assumes that, if the sentences in which descriptions occur are true, each description stands for an object, and the rest of the sentence expresses what holds of the object. To say this is to compare descriptions with (real) proper names; but at the same time the way in which descriptions stand for objects must be different from the way in which proper names stand for objects; indeed, the consideration of this leads to a breakdown of the idea that descriptions 'stand-for' at all.

This is most obvious for indefinite descriptions; but is also true of definite descriptions. A proper name will stand for its object because that object is called by that name; but a description, if it stands for its object, does so because the object satisfies it, which is clearly quite a different relation.

Further: If a proper name (i.e. what has the superficial grammar of a proper name) has in fact no bearer in the use that is being made of it, then nothing has been ascribed to any object by sentences in which it occurs; and so nothing has been said, truly or falsely. But if it has a bearer (i.e. if it has the use, and not merely the superficial grammar, of a proper name) then the sentence is false if what is predicated in it does not hold of that bearer. Now if a sentence like 'Some man has been on the Moon' is false, this is not because 'has been on the Moon' is false of some man—though if it is true, it is true because 'has been on the Moon' is true of some man. So, if we persist in thinking that the sentence would be made true by the fact that something holds of what the grammatical subject stands for, it turns out that its falsehood would not consist in the same thing's *not* holding of what the grammatical subject stands for.

When we turn to definite descriptions, it is easier to retain the comparison with proper names; hence Frege called definite descriptions proper names. But the comparison breaks down in various ways. The predicate occurring as part of a definite description must be uniquely true of something, if the description is to be taken as standing for anything; whereas a proper name stands for a bearer to which it has been assigned, without its being guaranteed, concerning any given unique description, that the bearer satisfies it. Hence we can give truth-conditions for statements containing definite descriptions regardless of whether the descriptions are vacuous or not.

It has been said (in the first instance by Frege) that the occurrence of a vacuous definite description in a sentence disqualifies that sentence from making a true or false statement. But this is unplausible except when the sentence is a simple one. A vacuous definite description can occur in a clause within a sentence without so disqualifying the whole sentence, e.g. 'Either he has no children or his first child's name is Hilary.' All this shews that the object, if there is one, satisfying a definite description, is not so designated by it that nothing could be truly or falsely said by a sentence containing the description if that object did not exist; whereas if Scott had never existed, the use of the word 'Scott' as the name of that famous author never could have existed either.

As a logical doctrine, Russell's Theory of Descriptions makes the contrast between definite descriptions and (ordinary) proper names which these considerations seem to demand. When doing logic, Russell always treats e.g. 'Scott' as a proper name, by contrast with descriptions like 'the author of Waverley'. His theory of knowledge, on the other hand, leads him to propound the less convincing part of the theory: that ordinary proper names, like 'Scott', are not the real proper names at all. A genuine proper name must have a bearer; this is a harmless point of logic; it becomes less harmless if it is rendered as: What a proper name stands for must exist. For this may lead us to the idea that the bearers of the only genuine proper names are existents not subject to Cartesian doubt (Russell's objects of immediate acquaintance—sense-data, etc.); or are eternal and changeless simples (Wittgenstein's 'objects').

Russell says that a definite description has no meaning by itself, but the whole sentence in which it occurs has a meaning. He means simply that a definite description does not function like a name. He puts the point in that obscure way because of his idea of what it is for a word or phrase to 'have meaning', namely: a word has meaning if it is a word with which one means an object; to mean an object one must be acquainted with it; for a word or phrase to have meaning, then, it is necessary for what we mean by it to exist. In accordance with this theory of meaning Russell passes from the truism that in order to understand a sentence we must know what each word means, to the doctrine that in judging or supposing we must be acquainted with each of the objects that the judgment or supposition is *really* about.

Thus, on Russell's view, if a description had 'meaning by itself', it would follow that what it stood for had some sort of being. In the *Principles of Mathematics* Russell had actually thought that there were entities 'meant' by descriptions, and called these entities 'denoting concepts'; not only definite descriptions, but such phrases as 'any number' in 'Any number is either odd or even', had denoting concepts as their 'meanings'. But what a proposition containing a description asserted would ordinarily be asserted not *of* the corresponding denoting concept, but of a term or complex of terms somehow connected with the denoting concept; e.g. it is not the denoting concept answering to the phrase 'any number' that is said to be odd or even. Russell's Theory of Descriptions represents an escape from this position; he adopted Frege's way of handling 'some' and 'all', indefinite descriptions and phrases like 'any number',[1] and further applied it, as Frege never did, to definite descriptions as well.

Frege's enquiries had already given the notion of proper names an importance for logic and the theory of truth which it had never

[1] *See* Chapter 11. cf. also *Philosophical Writings of Gottlob Frege* (Blackwell, 1952), pp. 13–14, 16–20, 35–8, 93.

had before. In Russell's theory it retains that importance, and at the same time comprises only logically simple signs: 'A "simple" symbol is one which has no parts that are symbols. Thus "Scott" is a simple symbol because though it has parts (namely separate letters), these parts are not symbols. On the other hand "the author of Waverley" is not a simple symbol because the separate words that compose the symbol are parts which are symbols.'[1] This account of the simplicity of proper names is correct; as also it is correct to say that the way a proper name contributes to the meaning of a sentence in which it occurs is simply that it stands for its bearer.

Russell analyses e.g. 'The author of Waverley drank port' as: 'For some x, x wrote Waverley and for all y, y wrote Waverley only if y=x, and x drank port'; such an analysis of sentences containing definite descriptions and other 'denoting phrases' excludes these from the class of signs that contribute to the meaning of sentences in which they occur by standing for their bearers. The denoting phrases disappear, and only the predicates (and proper names, if any) used in their construction play a part in the result of the analysis. In consequence, 'standing-for' is shewn to be attributable *only* to simple signs. 'Where,' Wittgenstein asked in a later writing, 'does language hook on to the world?' One place will be here, where the proper name stands for its bearer.

In Russell's doctrine, a simple sign's having a meaning consists in its standing for something; its meaning simply is the thing for which it stands; and 'simple signs' will include not only proper names of 'individuals', but also signs for 'universals'—i.e. for relations, and for non-relational properties (if there are any)—and perhaps signs for logical forms as well; and these other simple signs will equally have as their meanings the non-individual 'things' they are signs for. Now, after *Philosophical Investigations*, it is easy to distinguish between the two different elements of this doctrine which we have mentioned: (a) the doctrine of the simplicity of the proper name, and of its contributing to the meaning of the sentence precisely by standing for its bearer; and (b) the idea that the meaning of a name just *is* its bearer, or the meaning of a simple sign like

[1] *Introduction to Mathematical Philosophy*, p. 173.

'red' just *is* the quality with which we have immediate acquaintance. At the time when Russell wrote, these elements were inextricably conflated into one theory.

One of the most noteworthy features of Russell's doctrine is his rejection of the Fregean distinction between sense and reference.[1] This distinction is highly plausible and tempting; but as an instrument in the theory of truth it leads to great difficulties, and not to the solution of our problems. Frege held that all symbols—i.e. both 'proper names' and predicates—had 'sense', that some 'proper names' had reference as well, and that all predicates had reference, the reference of a predicate being what he termed a concept. (But he does not explain the distinction of sense from reference for simple predicates.[2]) An unasserted sentence (e.g. one occurring as a clause in another sentence) is for him a proper name; if it has reference, its reference is a truth-value. This raises the problem how it comes about that certain senses—namely those of sentences containing no vacuous proper names—are guaranteed to have reference.

On Russell's theory this problem does not arise; in any fully analysed sentence there will occur nothing but words whose meanings are present to us and are real things; for those meanings will just *be* the 'things' (including relations, properties, and logical forms signified by logical words and logical schemata) for which the words stand. In his theory, we may say, 'language reaches right up to reality', which is something we want to shew it doing.

But there are great defects in the theory as Russell states it, even if for the moment we allow him to identify the meaning of a name with its bearer. For Russell held that judgment and supposing are (different) relations in which the mind stands to a set of objects including a relation R; if R relates the objects other than R in this set, then the judgment or supposition is true, and if not it is false.

[1] His detailed criticisms were, however, partly based on misunderstanding: he wrongly assimilated Frege's views to what he had held in the *Principles of Mathematics*.

[2] For at least some complex predicates the distinction is easily made out: the two predicates 'killed Socrates' and 'killed the philosopher who was executed by a draught of hemlock' have different senses but the same reference.

This theory (a) 'does not make it impossible to judge a nonsense', as Wittgenstein complains at 5.5422; (b) fails to distinguish effectively between judging (or supposing) that aRb and that bRa; and (c) fails to explain negative judgments. For if when I judge that A is to the right of B I stand in the judging relation to A, B, and the relation *to the right of*, what happens when I judge that A is *not* to the right of B? Do I stand in the judging relation to A, B, *to the right of*, and *not*? Similar questions arise for the other logical constants, 'if', 'and', and 'or'.

This difficulty lies behind Wittgenstein's remark (3.42): 'Although the proposition can only determine a single region of logical space, still the whole of logical space must be given by it. Otherwise negation, the logical sum,[1] the logical product,[2] etc. would keep on introducing new elements—in co-ordination' (sc. with those previously introduced).

Wittgenstein avoids these difficulties, while retaining the idea that the meaning of a simple sign is its bearer, by giving a different account of propositions, judgments, and logical constants. On the other hand he accepts Russell's Theory of Descriptions in its purely logical aspect—in so far as it shews how the analysis of propositions into the complete statement of their truth-conditions is to be carried out for propositions containing definite descriptions. The statement of truth-conditions for a proposition containing a definite description thus includes a statement that there is one and only one object satisfying the description, i.e. a statement that for some x, ϕx, and, for all y, ϕy only if y=x.

Let us now suppose that we have a proposition 'A is corrupt'. Here 'A' appears in the argument place in the function 'x is corrupt'. Now let us consider the negation: 'A is not corrupt.' Can we distinguish between an external and an internal negation here—i.e. between taking this as the negation of the result of substituting 'A' for 'x' in 'x is corrupt' (external negation), and taking it as the result of substituting 'A' for 'x' in 'x is not corrupt' (internal negation)? If we cannot, then 'A' is a proper name; if we can, it is not. One sort of case where we can is where 'A' is, e.g. 'Some committee' or 'Any institution'. For these cases the point is readily seen (cf. Chapter 1,

[1] *p* or *q*. [2] *p* and *q*.

p. 35). But where 'A' is a definite description, the distinction between the internal and external negation still holds.

The question whether there must be simple signs in Russell's sense thus leads us on to the question whether there must be substitutions in 'x is corrupt' for which there is *no* distinction between internal and external negation. Now if 'A' is an ostensibly singular term, the distinction could arise only because the expression 'A' itself indicated certain truth-conditions.

A proper name never does this; either one has to be told *ad hoc* what, and what kind of thing, it is a proper name of; or one may glean this latter information from the predicates associated with the name, or guess it from custom: for example 'John' is customarily a masculine human name in English-speaking countries—though this does not mean that a man makes a mistake if he calls his sow 'John'.

Our question is: *Must* there be (at least the possibility of) proper names? And this question can be reformulated thus: Is it impossible that, for any given f, *every* proposition which is a value of fx should indicate truth-conditions C distinct from the conditions for the holding of the property f? Now the statement of the truth-conditions C will run: 'There is an x such that ϕx, and, for all y, ϕy only if y=x'. But this could not be true, unless *some* singular proposition of the form 'ϕb' were true. It might indeed be known, without our knowing any singular proposition of the form 'ϕb'; but if we claimed to know it we should be postulating, even if we did not know, a proposition of the form 'ϕb'.

Thus we have

(1) fA, where 'A' is of the form 'The ϕ'.

(2) There is an x such that ϕx, and, for all y, ϕy only if y=x.

(3) ϕb.

Now what do we postulate about the sign 'b' in this postulated proposition? Necessarily, that there is for it no distinction between ($\sim\phi$)b and $\sim$(ϕb). For if there were such a distinction, the proposition 'There is not an x such that ϕx' would in turn be ambiguous in its truth-conditions: it might require that every proposition got by substituting an expression of the kind 'b' in '($\sim\phi$)x' shall be true, or that every proposition got by substituting an expression of the kind 'b' in 'ϕx' shall be false. There would thus be two quite different ways in which '(Ex)ϕx' might be false, if the only substitutions for x in 'ϕx' were expressions 'b' such that 'ϕb' had different possible negations.

So much follows from the *logical* part of the Theory of Descriptions. This, however, does not lead us to 'simples'; for the theory in its logical aspect has nothing to do with any theory of reduction to simples. It only demands that such simple symbols as 'Parliament' shall be possible if such propositions as 'The body making laws for Great Britain is corrupt' are to make sense. The type of name that is postulated here is the type: *name of a body corporate*. A truth-condition for 'The British legislative body is corrupt' is 'There is an x such that x corporately makes laws for Great Britain'. The variable 'x' here ranges over bodies corporate.

If there were no such things as bodies corporate, there would be no proper names of them either; so it looks as if in that case 'There is an x such that x corporately makes laws for Great Britain' would lose its meaning. But in a world where there were no such things, it might still be possible to imagine them. For a body corporate, e.g., to *pass a measure by a large majority* means that men stand in certain relations to one another and do certain things. If there were no bodies corporate, someone might yet imagine certain men standing in these relations to one another, might give an imaginary proper name to the complex so formed, and might construct predicates that were to hold of the complex when the individuals standing in these relations did certain things. The proposition 'There is an x such that x corporately makes laws' would then after all not fail to have meaning.

Let us suppose that someone in a world without bodies corporate has imagined there being such things, and has constructed this proposition; there are now two quite different ways in which it can be false, though not the same two ways as we considered before. It is false in his world, because there are no bodies corporate at all there. But in a possible world where there *were* bodies corporate, there would be no distinction between 'All substitutions for "x" in "x corporately makes laws" are false' and 'All substitutions in "x does not corporately make laws" are true'; these propositions would both be true or both false together, and if they were true then 'There is an x such that x corporately makes laws' would be false.

Let us call the falsehood of this proposition in the world where there are no bodies corporate 'radical falsehood': the proposition is radically false because certain propositions about men are false—they do not stand in such relations or do such things.

The question arises: could there always be the possibility of radical, as opposed to ordinary, falsehood? It is clear that a 'radical falsehood' always depends on the possibility of an ordinary falsehood. Wittgenstein's starting-point is: We can construct propositions at will, without enquiry into any facts at all, and know what is the case *if* they are true. On the supposition that the question of 'radical falsehood' can always be raised, we should always have to distinguish between possible kinds of falsehood of our statements.

But then we could never determine the sense of the falsehood of a proposition, except on the supposition of the *truth* of some prior proposition; for otherwise we should each time have to consider the possibility of a radical falsehood, which must be explained in terms of the ordinary falsehood of a prior proposition. Then we might indeed start from the *truth* of certain propositions; but without this we could never know the sense of any. 'Whether one proposition made sense would depend on whether another one was true; so we should not be able to invent a picture of the world (true or false)' (2.0211–2).

Thus if we can construct propositions at will and know what is the case if they are true, without knowing what is true and what is false, it follows that there must be propositions incapable of what I have called 'radical' falsehood. That is to say, there must be names of simples which can only be named, and not *defined* by a description as Parliament is, and whose existence is guaranteed. 'The demand for the possibility of the simple signs is the demand that sense shall be determinate' (3.23).

Here the 'simple signs' are not the 'simple symbols' of the Theory of Descriptions, in its purely logical aspect as presented by Russell. Wittgenstein shares with Russell the idea that the meaning of a name is its bearer: but in him this is not noticeably based on the British empiricist epistemology that influences Russell. We have, rather, a Frege-like argument: Unless names have bearers, there is no truth or falsehood. But if you *always* distinguish a sense and a reference in names, as you must for a name like 'Parliament', the connection between sense and truth-value becomes obscure. For then the sense of a name will present a reference if something satisfies the description in which that sense might be set forth, i.e. if something is *true*; now this truth must be expressible by combining a name and a predicate; and unless names are somewhere nailed to reality without the mediation of senses which hold true of objects, that relation between sentences and reality which constitutes their truth will in no way have been explained.

3

NEGATION: (1) THE LOGICIANS' DEFINITION OF 'NOT P'

'Everyone is unwise' is a negation of 'everyone is wise', but it is not what logicians call *the* negation of it; in logic books, when the sign for 'not' is introduced, we are told that 'not p' is '*the* proposition that is true when p is false and false when p is true'. 'Everyone is unwise' is not certainly true if 'Everyone is wise' is false; hence it is not *the* negation of 'Everyone is wise'. This was the point already noticed by Aristotle in the *De Interpretatione*.

Such a definition of 'not p' as is found in many logic books may make us ask (rather in the manner of Frege) what right anyone has to give such a definition. I can define something as *the* so-and-so, only if I am justified in being sure, first that there is *a* so-and-so, and second that there is only one. If I have no such assurance, it is not certain that I am succeeding in defining anything. How, then, am I assured that there is one, and only one, proposition that is true when p is false, and false when p is true?

It might seem that we could say: It is evident that a proposition has two truth-values, as a coin has two sides; and we might think of truth-functions as like bets on the results of tossing coins. Thus if one coin is tossed once, there are two possible bets, which can be represented as follows:

Coin	*Bet 1*	*Bet 2*
H	W	L
T	L	W

in a table in which H and T stand for heads and tails, and W and L for win and lose. This could be considered to correspond to the following truth-table:

p	p	~p
T	T	F
F	F	T

The analogy of course holds for the whole range of truth-functions. For example, if we have two coins, A and B, we could set forth one possible bet as follows:

A	B	
H	H	W
H	T	L
T	H	W
T	T	W

Here the bet that the coins, in a single toss of both together, will fall so that either A is tails or B is heads, corresponds to the truth-function

p	q		or alternatively
T	T	T	T
T	F	F	T
F	T	T	F
F	F	T	T

that is to say: to ~p v q, or alternatively, to ~q v p; which, depends on whether we assimilate 'Heads' or 'Tails' to 'True'.

The most striking thing about this analogy is that when we set forth the table of bets on the toss of a coin, we put different symbols in the columns that display the bets from those we put in the columns of possible results of the toss, whereas in the truth-table we used the same signs in all three columns. The question arises with what right, or on what grounds, or again, with a view to expressing what, we use the same symbols in all the columns of the truth-table, which we should not think of doing in all the columns of the betting tables.

Consider the explanations of propositions and truth-functions, or logical constants, which are commonly found in logic books. It is usual for us to be told: first, propositions are whatever can be either true or false; second, propositions can be combined in certain ways to form further propositions; and third, in examining these combinations, i.e. in developing the truth-functional calculus, we are not interested in the internal structure of the combined propositions.[1]

Such explanations raise certain questions: e.g. has the internal structure of the propositions, which does not concern us when we study truth-functions, anything to do with the property of being true or false? Again, is the property of being true or false, which belongs to the truth-functions, the very same property as the property of being true or false that belongs to the propositions whose internal structure does not interest us? And, finally, if that is so, is it to be regarded as an ultimate fact that propositions combine to form further propositions, much as metals combine to form alloys which still display a good many of the properties of metals?

In short, is there not an impression as it were of logical chemistry about these explanations? It is this conception that Wittgenstein opposes in the *Tractatus* at 6.111: 'Theories that make a proposition of logic appear substantial are always wrong. It might be thought, for example, that the words "true" and "false" denote two properties among other properties, and then it would look like a remarkable fact that every proposition possesses one of these properties. This now looks no more a matter of course than the proposition "all roses are either red or yellow" would sound, even if it were true.'

Logical calculi are sometimes described as essentially sets of marks with rules for manipulating them. For example Lewis and Langford (*Symbolic Logic*, p. 227) say: 'Whatever more it may be, the matrix method at least is a kind of game which we play with recognizable marks, according to certain rules.' They then make some

[1] *See* e.g. Hilbert and Ackermann, *Mathematical Logic*, p. 3.

remarks concerning an extract for a table for pIq (which might have the *logical* interpretation p⊃q, but of course need not):

p	q	pIq
1	1	1
1	0	0

They rightly assert that such a table need not have 'any "logical" significance'; p and q may be 'any kind of things'. What is required on their view is that in some game or other there should be 'an operation or move, pIq, which according to the rules can be taken when p has the property A, only if q also has the property A'; and in that case the table will tell us that if p has the property A, and pIq is an allowable move, then q must have A. The logical interpretation will then consist in taking the property A, expressed by the figure '1', to be truth, and the property expressed by the figure '0' to be falsehood, and reading 'pIq' as 'p⊃q'.

The animus behind such a view as this is a desire to get rid of the notion of 'logical truth' in the mysterious character that it assumes to someone with an empiricist outlook. But the argument presented by Lewis and Langford fails, and, by the way in which it fails, helps us to see the importance of the fact that we use the same signs, 'T' and 'F', or '1' and '0', in all the columns of a truth-table. For—as has been remarked by Geach[1]—there is an inconsistency here in the interpretation of the figure 1, if p and q may be 'any kind of things'. As regards p and q, the figure '1' is taken to stand for some property A, but as regards pIq it is taken to stand for the property of being an allowable move in a certain game. This is inconsistent unless A *is* the property of being an allowable move—and that is not necessary.

That it is not necessary is clearly seen if we take a simple non-logical interpretation of the table. Let the figures '1' and '0' connote the presence and the absence of an hereditary property A, and let 'pIq' mean 'offspring by p out of q'. Then the table will have no reference to moves in any game. It will state that the trait A is present in the offspring, when it is present in the sire, if and only if

[1] *Ifs and Ands*, Analysis, Vol. 9, 1948–9. This and the succeeding two paragraphs are adapted from this article.

it is also present in the dam: a good example of what Wittgenstein would call a 'substantial' piece of information. Note that here pIq is not a 'move in a game' at all—any more than p and q are; pIq is an animal.

Now though, as this example shows, you need not interpret the figures '1' and '0' to mean that moves in a game are respectively allowed and forbidden, it is of course perfectly permissible to do so. But in that case p and q cannot be 'any kind of things' but must be moves in the game, like pIq. The table will then be equivalent to the following sentence: 'If p is an allowable move, then q is an allowable move if and only if pIq is also an allowable move.' And here the sign 'I' does not belong to the terminology of any special game, like 'Kt' in chess; it expresses what we may fittingly call a logical relation of the move pIq to the moves p and q, so that the significance of the notation 'pIq' is after all 'logical'.

Now 'If p is an allowable move, then q is an allowable move if and only if pIq is an allowable move' at least sounds like a substantial piece of information about a game; at any rate if one can specify p, q, and pIq independently as moves: p might be a diagonal move of a certain piece on a squared board, q a move of another piece parallel with an edge of the board, and 'pIq' the name given (we won't ask why, for the moment) to a move by yet another piece along one of the edges of the board. Then the information 'If you can move this piece diagonally you can move this piece along the edge of the board if, and only if, you can move this piece parallel with one of the edges' might either be a rule of the game, or inferable from the rules of the game.

If, however, we now do ask why moving this piece along the edge of the board should be symbolized by a sign mentioning those two other moves, then we can answer by saying that

p	q	
1	1	1
1	0	0

defines a possible allowability in terms of given allowabilities, and 'pIq' is a notation in which this allowability is set forth: that, and that alone, is the meaning of this notation. Then the substantial information as far as this game is concerned is that there do exist some moves whose allowability is so conditioned, and that the move along the edge of the board is in fact one of them; but that any move describable as pIq is allowable, if p is allowable, if and only if q is also allowable, is not a 'substantial' piece of information.[1]

Similarly, if we revert to the analogy of tossing coins, we set forth part of the betting table we have already considered:

Coin A	*Coin B*	*Bet: A tails or B heads*
H	H	W
H	T	L

and it is not a substantial piece of information that this is a possible bet on the result of a toss of two coins, each with two possible sides to come uppermost. Nor is it informative to say that this *is* the bet 'A tails or B heads'; that is simply another way of writing what is already written down in the WL column; one could simply point to the column and say: That's my bet.

And so Wittgenstein says that such a sign as

p	q	
T	T	T
T	F	F
F	T	F
F	F	F

or, assuming a standard convention for the p and q columns, '(TFFF) (p,q)' *is* a propositional sign: we find this statement at 4.442. '(TFFF) (p,q)' is just another way of writing 'p.q'.

This is the explanation of the symbolism introduced at 5.5:

$$(- - - - - - \mathrm{T})\ (\xi, \ldots\ldots)$$

The Greek letter ξ is a variable whose value is a proposition; the

[1] The reader must be careful, in reading this passage, to distinguish between 'pIq' and pIq. pIq is a move in the game, 'pIq' a notation for the move.

dots after it indicate a set of such variables of unspecified length. The dashes in the left-hand bracket indicate an absence of T's in the truth-table, however long this may be: its length in any given case will depend on how many propositions are indicated in the right-hand bracket. The point is that only the bottom row of the matrix has T set against it: this is the case in which *all* the propositions indicated in the right-hand bracket are false; this combination is to stand at the bottom, whichever of various possible conventions is adopted for arranging the other possible combinations of truth-values in the matrix. Thus Wittgenstein's formula '(– – – – – – – T) (ξ^1 . . . . . .)' is the negation of all the propositions in the right-hand bracket.

Now in the coin-tossing case, the 'substantial' information is that the toss of a coin has two possibilities, heads and tails. And as we have seen, this substantial fact has an analogue in the opening explanations of logic books: that propositions are what can be true or false. We might say that for coin-tossing purposes a coin has only two possibilities of falling: if a coin e.g. stood on its edge when it reached the floor, that wouldn't count as a toss. And similarly if (for whatever reason) a sentence hasn't got a truth-value, it doesn't count for making statements with or for operating the truth-functional calculus with.

Frege allows such sentences: if a sentence is a fiction, it has not got a truth-value; and it is a fiction if it contains empty names. It can still have a perfectly good 'sense', but not have a truth-value. In our day, Mr. P. F. Strawson has also introduced a concept of a sentence's having a sense, which is not sufficient to guarantee that if it is uttered a statement is thereby made. We know its sense, if we know in what circumstances it *could* be used to make a statement. Now, apart from sentences containing fictitious proper names, Frege found his view inconvenient; he regarded the possibility of constructing such sentences as a defect in the language of (*a priori*) science.[2] So when

[1] This is used rather than 'p' because 'p' is generally used for an elementary proposition, and there is no requirement here that the value of ξ be elementary.

[2] In an empirical science, such as astronomy, the possibility cannot be regarded as a defect of language, or legislated away. e.g. at one time it was thought that there was an extra planet, which was called 'Vulcan'. On Frege's view propositions about Vulcan could not have a truth-value.

in developing the foundations of mathematics he needed to use a descriptive phrase which as ordinarily interpreted might have no reference, he used an artificial reinterpretation to guarantee that it had a reference;[1] and this artificiality, as Russell remarks, is an objection to his procedure. Mr. Strawson's own suggestion has not been sufficiently worked out for us to estimate its value.

It is well known that Russell and Wittgenstein were on the other side of this fence; for Wittgenstein 'having a sense' was one and the same thing with being true-or-false. We have already seen this at 3.24: 'The proposition in which a complex is mentioned does not become nonsensical if the complex does not exist, but simply false.' And we see it again at 4.063, where he develops an illustration of the concept of truth by a black spot on white paper: black corresponds to true and white to false. If you indicate a point on the surface, that is like pointing to what Frege calls a 'thought', or the sense of a sentence; and you are, of course, pointing to something that is in fact either black or white. But, Wittgenstein says, the point at which the illustration goes lame is this: you can indicate a point on a sheet of paper without so much as having a notion of black and white; what would correspond to this would be indicating a thought without so much as having a notion of true and false: 'but to a proposition without a sense there corresponds nothing, for a proposition doesn't designate an object with the properties called "true" and "false";' as, say, the description of a point designates an object with the properties called 'black' and 'white'. That is to say, unless the proposition is already something true or false, he calls it something 'without sense'.

Again, at 4.064, we find Wittgenstein saying: 'Every proposition must *already* have a sense; assertion cannot give it one.' Since this is an attack upon Frege, it may well confuse a reader; for of course Frege would agree that every (well-formed) sentence must already have a sense! But Wittgenstein holds that what already has a sense

[1] In school mathematics one is told that '$\frac{x}{y}$' does not mean any number when $y=0$; a reinterpretation in Frege's style might stipulate that when $y\neq 0$, $\frac{x}{y}$ is the number z such that $zy=x$, and when $y=0$, $\frac{x}{y}=x$.

must already be true or false; he is attacking Frege's idea that in judging we 'advance from a thought to a truth-value'.[1]

Wittgenstein remained on this side of the fence all his life; for in the very passage of *Philosophical Investigations* in which he attacked the ideas about complexes which he expounded in the *Tractatus*, he asked: 'Am I really prepared in advance to say what, and how much, has got to turn out untrue before I give up my proposition about Moses as *false*?' The kind of thing he has been considering has been facts that, taken together, would tend to shew that there was no such person as Moses; and he spoke of giving up the proposition about Moses, not as neither true nor false, but as false.

It will be worth while to say a few things about the Frege-Strawson side of the fence. First, Frege was sure that a well-formed sentence whose names were not empty had a truth-value. But is it not strange to be sure of that? Is it not as if there were a great metal wall with holes in it, and we had some way of casting metal objects, and were absolutely certain that each object that was properly cast would fit into a hole in the wall one way up or the other (the well-formed proposition or its negation is true) although no connection had been shewn between the principles of casting objects and the character of the metal wall? The fact that Frege's account makes things look like this is a sure sign that he has gone wrong, like the accounts of 'true' and 'false' which make 'Every proposition is either true or false' like 'Every rose is either red or yellow'. Frege's reply to this would be that a sentence is only well-formed if the concepts it employs are sharply defined, and a concept is sharply defined if it is determined for every object whether it falls under that concept or not. The problem now assumes the form: how does it come about that we can form concepts for which this is determined, without any reference to the facts?

Secondly, Frege actually said that the truth-conditions determine the sense of a proposition. He specifies the truth-conditions, and therefore (since he is working in an *a priori* discipline) the truth-value, which on his theory is also the reference, of any well-formed formula in his system; he then adds, as if to anticipate the

[1] *See* 'Sense and Reference', in *Philosophical Writings of Gottlob Frege*, p. 65.

objection that he has only specified the reference and not the sense, that the sense of such a formula is the sense of this: that its truth-conditions are fulfilled. And to this, *mutatis mutandis*, we may see a correspondence in Mr. Strawson's 'knowing in what circumstances the sentence could be used to make a statement'. The propositions embodying the truth-conditions, or describing the circumstances in which a sentence could be used to make a statement, must themselves be either true or false, or require explanation in terms of further truth-conditions, or further circumstances. In view of this, the Frege-Strawson position on the possibility of sentences without truth-value appears to be a waste of time: in such an account the concept of 'sense' is not divorced from those of truth and falsehood; it is merely determined that when certain of the truth-conditions of a proposition are false we are to say that 'nothing either true or false has been said'.

We have observed that the most striking difference between the coin-tossing tables and the truth-tables is that in the former we use different symbols in setting out the possible results of coin-tossing and the possible bets on these results. Now let us suppose that we have a coin with 'win' written on one side and 'lose' on the other, so that we said that we bet on the coin's coming up 'win' or 'lose' rather than 'heads' and 'tails'. Then a bet that the coin would 'win' —a bet, so to speak, in agreement with the coin—on the one hand, and a bet that the coin would lose, would be exactly comparable to the two truth-functions of a single proposition:

p		
T	T	F
F	F	T

The objection immediately arises that while we have a good sense for 'winning' and 'losing' in connection with a *bet* on whether the coin will fall one side up or the other, there really is no sense in these terms as applied to the sides of the coin themselves, except that we *happen* to write this sign on one side and that on the other. The signs are not really the same; any more than 'jam' is the same word in English and in Latin. Now that may be so: but we have in fact already encountered a parallel difficulty in connection with using the word 'true' for the elementary propositions and for the truth-functions. It may be intuitively obvious that there is no equivocation; and it is certainly extremely natural to give the explanations found in the logic books and then simply get on with the calculus. But our questions were reasonable ones; if there is no way of answering them, and we have just to rely on our intuition, that is of itself an important fact—at any rate, it is important for philosophy.

The *Tractatus*, however, does attempt to give an answer to these questions other than that the correctness of these two uses of the words 'true' and 'false' is intuitively obvious. I opened by raising the question: If we offer a definition of 'not p' as 'that proposition which is true when p is false and false when p is true' how can this be justified if we are not assured that there is such a proposition, and only one? Now grounds are given for saying that there is only one such proposition at 5.513: 'It could be said that what is common to all symbols that assert p as well as q, is the proposition "p.q." What is common to all symbols that either assert p or assert q, is the proposition "p v q".

'And in this way it can be said: Two propositions are opposed to one another, if they have nothing in common, and: Every proposition has only one negative, because there is only one proposition which is wholly outside it.'

In the first of these paragraphs, we must understand that it is the propositions 'p.q' and 'p v q' that are being explained in terms of what is common to a class of symbols. We have already seen Wittgenstein saying (3.341) that the essential thing about a symbol, or the *real symbol*, is what all symbols that do the same job have in common. If then there is anything that a set of propositions all say, then what is common to that set of propositions he calls the *real symbol* for the thing that they all say. So you might say that a set of propositions, 'A is red', 'A is green', 'A is blue', etc., have something they *all* say, namely: 'A is coloured.' And the 'real symbol' for 'A is coloured' will be what is common to the propositions 'A is red', 'A is green', 'A is blue', etc.

Now any set of independent propositions has something that they all say; what this is is brought out by writing out a truth-table where all places but the bottom are marked 'T', the bottom place having F in it opposite the row of F's of the matrix. This truth-table specifies a proposition, which is made true by the truth of any one of the components; hence I call it something that they *all* say. And according to Wittgenstein's dictum, the 'real symbol' for this will be what is common to them all. But the proposition in question is of course the disjunction of them all: and hence the 'real symbol' for e.g. p v q is what is common to all propositions that either assert p or assert q.

How the common thing about a set of symbols, and hence the 'real symbol', is to be described is a matter of which the *Tractatus* gives an account in the range of entries under 3.31, that is to say, 3.31–3.318, and there is further matter relevant to the specification of *sets of propositions* at 5.501. Let us assume that the account is satisfactory. For our present purpose is to shew how Wittgenstein proposes to justify our assurance that every proposition has only one negative.

'Two propositions are opposed to one another if they have nothing in common.' That is to say, if there is nothing that they both say. In this sense 'The King of France is bald' and 'The King of France is not bald' are not opposed to one another (if the latter is the result of substituting 'The King of France' for 'x' in 'x is not bald'), for there is something that they both say. This comes out in the fact that 'The King of France is bald or the King of France is not bald' may not hold, namely if there is no King of France; the proposition therefore asserts something, viz. that some one of the situations in which it would hold is actual; it asserts something because these situations are not an exhaustive list of all possible situations; it excludes the situation in which it would not hold.

He goes on to say: 'Every proposition has only one negative, because there is only one proposition that lies wholly outside it.' Let us test this by supposing that there might be two. *Ex hypothesi*, these two must have different senses, i.e. it must be possible for one to hold and the other not. Let us write them as not-p (1) and not-p (2). Then the disjunction of p and not-p (1) could be false, if what held were not-p (2). So the disjunction of p and not-p (1) does assert something, and there is something asserted by both p and not-p (1), namely that some one of the situations in which the disjunction would hold is actual. It follows that there can be at most *one* proposition that has 'nothing in common' with any given proposition. There can of course be many propositional *signs* for this proposition, but their sense will all be the same.

That there can be at most one proposition of this character for any given proposition does not shew that there is one; and we must next shew how this is made out in the *Tractatus*.

4

NEGATION: (2) THE PICTURE THEORY

We have been troubled by the procedure of the logic books in e.g. placing the same signs, T and F, under the signs of the elementary proposition in the truth-table and in the final column, and by the justifications of this procedure, which consist in quasi-factual pronouncements. Let us now consider remedying this procedure. I adopt two new signs, P and N, which mean 'Positive' and 'Negative', which I put under the signs for the elementary propositions:

p		
P	T	F
N	F	T

The proposition which is an element in a truth-function is thus introduced as having two senses, the positive and the negative, rather than two truth-values, true and false.

Now there is actually some foundation for looking at it like this, in the *Tractatus* itself. At 4.463 Wittgenstein writes: 'The proposition, the picture, the model, in the negative sense are like a solid body, which restricts the free movements of another; in the positive sense, like the space limited by solid substance, in which a body may be placed.' Here at any rate a proposition, as well as a picture or model, is conceived as something that can have both a positive and a negative sense.

As far as concerns a picture, this is quite reasonable. It is in fact connected with one of the objections that it is most natural to feel to Wittgenstein's 'picture' theory of the position. A picture is not like a proposition: it doesn't say anything. A picture is not an assertion that something like it is to be found somewhere in the world, whereas in a proposition something is *said to be the case*. If we accept Wittgenstein's dictum at 4.022 that 'A proposition *shews* how things are *if* it is true. And it *says* that they are so', we might say: 'Just this shews the difference between a proposition and a picture; for while a picture may be said to *shew* how things are, *if* there is something it is a correct representation of, it certainly does not *say* that that is how things are; the most that one could grant would be that we could *use* the picture *in* saying how things are: we could hold the picture up and ourselves say: "This is how things are." '

Now in fact this is Wittgenstein's point. For in order to be able to do this in a quite straightforward sense, it is necessary that the elements of the picture should be correlated with objects.

For example, here is a picture:

and if I have correlated the right-hand figure with a man A, and the left-hand figure with a man B, then I can hold the picture up and say: 'This is how things are.' But I can just as well hold the picture up and say: 'This is how things aren't.'

If you could not do this with, say, the figures drawn or painted on a piece of paper, once they had been correlated with actual people or objects, then what was on the paper would not be a picture, but a set of figures each of which was correlated with some object.

I may for example draw a figure here

and call it 'Plato'; and then draw another figure here

and call it 'Socrates'; the two figures do not together constitute a picture, because although of course there is a relation between them—they are, say, a certain distance apart on a single leaf—this relation is non-significant. Whereas in the drawing of the two men fencing the relation of the ink strokes constituting the drawing of the first man and those constituting the drawing of the second man was significant.

The isolated figures labelled 'Plato' and 'Socrates' each consist of strokes in significant relationship, and hence it seems reasonable to speak of correlating such figures, one with one person, another with another. But if I just put a single stroke

/

and then another stroke

/

the sense that there was in saying 'correlate the first mark with one person and the second with another' would vanish. If someone said this, we should wait for something to be done with the strokes; we might think that this announcement was a preparation for something; unless it is that it is not anything at all. Suppose I said: 'That door stands for Dante and that table for Bertrand Russell'. My audience would, if anything, look at me enquiringly and say: 'Well?' And here 'Well?' means 'Do something to shew the point of this'; and *that* means 'Let something else come into such a relationship with this door, or again with this table, that the terms in relation represent something.' We could say: 'Only in the connections that make up the picture can the elements of the picture stand for objects.'

The picture-theory of the proposition is that the proposition in the positive sense says: 'This is how things are' and in the negative sense says: 'This is how things aren't'—the '*this*' in both cases being the same: the comparison is a comparison with a picture of the 'this' in question. It is because of the character of the 'this' that there is the *possibility* of saying 'it's how things are' or 'it's how things aren't'. And this character is in pictures, ordinary pictures, themselves—all that is required for the possibility to be actualized is that their figures be correlated with objects. This begins to tell us why Wittgenstein says at 2.182 that 'Every picture is *also* a logical picture'; and at 2.1514 that 'the picturing relation consists of the co-ordinations of the elements of the picture and of the things'.

The quite straightforward possibility of doing this depends on the correlations' having been made; now this correlation is in one way quite external. The picture of two men fencing was intelligible as a picture, without our making any correlations of the figures with individual men. We might compare to this picture, without individual correlations, what Wittgenstein at 3.24 calls the 'proto-picture' occurring in the generality notation: the 'xRy', for example, in '(Ex)(y)xRy'.

What I have called the externality of the correlations between the elements of a picture and actual objects is an important feature of Wittgenstein's account. Giancarlo Colombo, S.J., the Italian translator of the *Tractatus*, commented on Wittgenstein's theory of the 'isomorphism', as it is called, between language and the world, that it was difficult to see why a described fact should not be regarded as itself a description of the proposition that would normally be said to describe it, rather than the other way round. And as far as concerns the internal features of proposition and fact, this is a strong point; for all the internal features are supposed to be identical in the proposition (or describing fact) and the described fact.

But after having stated at 2.15 that the way the elements are connected in the picture is the same as the way it sets forth the things as being connected, Wittgenstein goes on to compare it to a ruler which you set up against an object (2.1512–2.15121) and then says: (2.1513) 'According to this conception, the picture must have in addition the depicting relation which makes it into a picture';[1] and, as we have already seen, this depicting relation consists of the correlations with objects (2.1514).

Thus there are two distinct features belonging to a picture (in the ordinary sense of 'picture'): first, the relation between the elements of the picture; and second, the correlations of the elements in the picture with things outside the picture; and as we have seen, the first feature must belong to a picture before the second one can; only if significant relations hold among the elements of the picture *can* they be correlated with objects outside so as to stand for them. The correlating is not something that the picture itself does; it is something *we* do.

We see this at 5.4733, where Wittgenstein says: 'Frege says: Every well-formed proposition must have a sense; and I say: Every possible proposition is well-formed, and if it doesn't make sense, this can only come of our not having supplied any reference for some of its component parts.' What Wittgenstein means by 'Every possible proposition is well-formed' is that the relations that must hold between the elements if a sentence is to be a sentence at all must be there also in any nonsensical sentence, if you could make this have a perfectly good sense just by changing the kind of reference that some part of the sentence had. Here it is 'we' who 'give' a sign its reference.

This is why at 3.13 Wittgenstein says that 'A proposition has in it everything that a projection has; but it hasn't got the projected thing in it; so it has the possibility of the projected thing in it, but not the very thing itself: And so the proposition does not yet contain its sense; what it does contain is the possibility of expressing that

[1] Ogden's rendering of this sentence: 'the representing relation . . . also belongs to the picture' can be misleading. There is evidence in Ramsey's review of the *Tractatus* (since Ramsey helped with the translation) that it was intended in an incorrect sense. Ramsey says that the elements 'are co-ordinated with the objects by the representing relation which belongs to the picture' (*Foundations of Mathematics*, p. 271). This interpretation throws Wittgenstein's quite straightforward idea into obscurity; the sentence has no such obscurity for educated native speakers of German.

sense. . . . It contains the *form* of its sense, but not its content.'[1] The reason why the proposition doesn't 'contain its sense' is that the correlations are made by us; we mean the objects by the components of the proposition in 'thinking its sense': this is part of what is meant at 3.11: 'The method of projection is the thinking of the sense of the proposition.' It is we who 'use the sensibly perceptible signs as a projection of a possible state of affairs'; we do this by using the elements of the proposition to stand for the objects whose possible configuration we are reproducing in the arrangement of the elements of the proposition. This is what Wittgenstein means by calling the proposition a picture. It is at any rate clear enough that we could use a picture in this way.

Now, confining ourselves to pictures, it is also clear that if we 'think[2] the sense of the picture' by correlating its elements with actual objects, we can in fact think it in either of *two* ways: namely either as depicting what is the case, or as depicting what isn't the case. That is to say, there are two senses which we can 'think' in connection with the picture. For it is the very same picture we hold up if we wish to say that *it* holds or that *it* doesn't hold. Or again, if I hold up a picture and say 'If I correlate the elements of this picture with things, I can *say* something by holding it up', someone might reply: There are two things you could assert in holding the picture up: first the existence, and second the non-existence, of that situation which is represented by the picture so soon as its elements are correlated with objects. And the difference between the two is not that the relations between the elements are taken to be different; on the contrary, they are exactly the same.

It is clear that one must convey *what* situation one is saying does not exist, and this will be conveyed precisely by the picture depicting that situation. No other *picture* could be involved: you could not for example make a *picture* of the situation's *not* existing. We must be

[1] Wittgenstein's use of 'projection' is a metaphorical extension of the mathematical use, which may be explained thus: 'The drawing of straight lines through every point of a given figure, so as to produce a new figure each point of which corresponds to a point of the original figure.' The new figure is also said to be a *projection of* the original one, which is *projected into* it (cf. *The Shorter Oxford Dictionary*).

[2] This is a Germanism which it seems necessary to retain in English.

careful not to confuse what is not the case with what is the case instead of it; if you tried to make a picture of a situation's *not* existing you would only make a picture of what did exist instead of it. The only exception to this is when we have the convention that not shewing something shews that the thing does not exist: as when a map shews that no large river passes through Birmingham by *not* shewing a river passing through Birmingham.

These, then, are the reasons for speaking of a picture as having—or rather being capable of being given—a positive and a negative sense. The two senses are integral to the picture, once the correlations have been established. Certainly a picture whose 'sense' is 'thought' one way or the other, as I have described, *is* a propositional sign.

What is mysterious about negation is that something's *not* being the case should be capable of being something that *is* the case;[1] and it is a peculiarity of a picture of something's being the case that it can be taken as presenting us with something that is the case by being a *picture of what is not the case*. In his notebooks, Wittgenstein speaks of logical constants as giving the method of projection of the proto-picture in the proposition. I think this conception is not discarded in the *Tractatus*.

In the course of his researches prior to writing the *Tractatus*, Wittgenstein invented what he called the a-b notation. He proposed to write a proposition like this:

a p b

the a and b being what he called the 'two poles' of the proposition. This notation has survived in the *Tractatus* at 6.1203, except that he writes T and F instead of a and b. But we could represent the propositional sign that is a picture (of the most ordinary kind) in the same way:

[1] cf. *Philosophical Investigations*, §429: 'The agreement, the harmony, of thought and reality consists in this: if I say falsely that something is *red*, then, for all that, it isn't *red*.' The problem is the ancient one of how a false proposition makes sense.

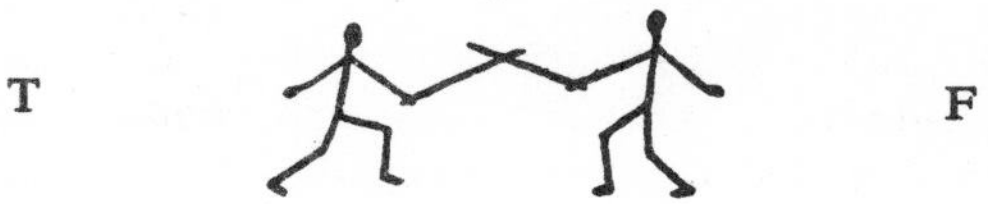

T F

This rendering of the picture become proposition would stress the fact that it has acquired two 'poles', or senses in which it can be thought, by having the drawn figures correlated with actual men.

Now the question is: does this conception give us what is essential to propositions, so that it is at all plausible to say that all propositions have this character?

I believe that the most that we can say is that the bi-polarity of the picture, of the occurrence of *one* picture in two senses, has a very striking analogy in the fact that if we have a proposition, and insert a 'not' into it, then *what* is being denied is exactly *what* the original proposition said. In negating a proposition we use the propositional sign to form another, and we tend to feel that both *say* something: and hence want an account that would justify this feeling. Both propositions *mention* exactly the same things in the same relation to one another. The picture-proposition we have imagined gives us a very clear idea of structures for which these points hold. And it is also true that the non-existence of a configuration of things is a clear and intelligible idea. What constitutes the truth and falsehood of the picture-proposition; its opposed positive and negative senses; its possession of these senses independently of whether it is true or false (i.e. of *which* truth-value it has)—all this is extremely intelligible: and what is intelligible here is precisely the *logical* character of the picture-proposition. But is it not the logical character that marks a proposition as such and that we want clarified? Something that seems to make this really clear might rather convincingly be taken to shew the essential character of a proposition.

So far as I can see, these are the real grounds for being struck even to the point of conviction by this account. It adds to its persuasiveness that it was capable of being further, and beautifully, thought out, and that it seemed to offer a solution to many problems, and finally even give a 'way of seeing the world rightly'. There are indeed serious difficulties about it; nevertheless, we shall understand the *Tractatus* best if we let ourselves succumb to the attractiveness of this idea, assume its correctness, and follow up its consequences throughout the *Tractatus*.

Every picture-proposition has two senses, in one of which it is a description of the existence, in the other of the non-existence, of a configuration of objects; and it is that by being a projection. It is the peculiarity of a projection that from it and the method of projection you can tell what is projected; the latter need not physically exist, though the points in space that it would occupy must. The idea of a projection is therefore peculiarly apt for explaining the character of a proposition as making sense independently of the facts: as intelligible before you know whether it is true; as something concerning which you can ask *whether* it is true, and know what you are asking before you know the answer.

If this explanation can be made to stick it will make the character of a proposition completely clear. For supposing TpF and TqF to be picture-propositions, then someone who says 'TpF' will be saying (let us suppose) that the situation pictured by 'p' exists; he can say it does not exist by reversing the T and F poles of 'TpF'—a procedure represented by Wittgenstein with: 'F-TpF-T'. The diagram

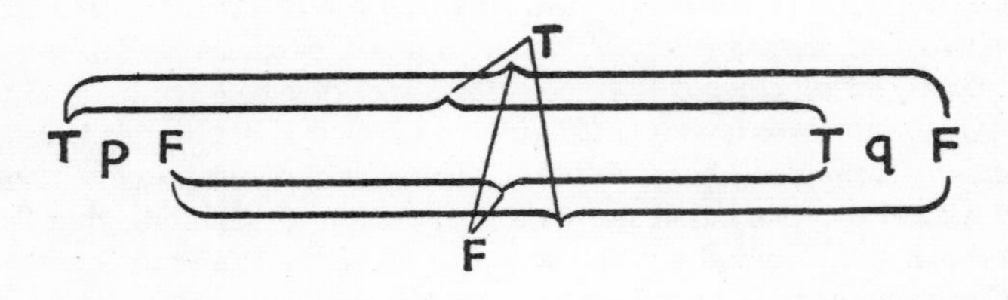

gives a picture-proposition, whose T pole is joined to a line joining the two T poles, and also to a line joining the two F poles, of 'TpF' and 'TqF', and whose F pole is joined to a line joining the T pole of 'TpF' with the F pole of 'TqF', and again to a line joining the F pole of 'TpF' with the T pole of 'TqF'. This proposition is true if the situations pictured by 'p' and 'q' both exist, or again if neither exists; otherwise false. This way of writing the propositional sign brings it out that nothing is mentioned but the objects correlated with the elements of 'p' and 'q' and no configurations introduced except those set forth in 'p' and 'q'.

The propositional sign written here in diagram form is the same proposition as what we would most commonly write $(p.q) \vee (\sim p.\sim q)$. This brings out why Wittgenstein says: 'The structure of the fact consists of the structures of the elementary situations' (2.034); 'The picture presents . . . the existence and non-existence of elementary situations' (2.11); 'The truth-conditions determine the play left to the facts by the proposition' (4.463); 'A proposition may be an incomplete picture of a particular state of affairs' (in this case, say, the state of affairs that neither p nor q) 'but it is always *a* complete picture' (5.156). For his idea was that definiteness of sense consists in this: a proposition may indeed leave a great deal open, but it is clear *what* it leaves open.

We must now return to the fact that a picture (in the ordinary sense) becomes a proposition the moment we correlate its elements with actual things. To shew this, I draw it shewing the T-F poles that it gets directly the correlation is made:

T  F

We must always remember the condition for the possibility of the correlation: namely that the arrangement of the ink strokes themselves is significant, is capable of picturing a situation *if* the correlations are made.[1]

[1] There is something that I slur over here for purposes of a first rough exposition: and that is the difference between the significant relations of the mere ink strokes, and the relations of the drawn members of the drawn figures and of the drawn figures among themselves. This corresponds to the difference between the significant relations between the sensibly perceptible signs, and the relations between the *symbols*. *See* 3.326.

Now, that some arrangement of shapes on a surface is capable of being a projection of another arrangement of shapes on a surface is obvious from their both being arrangements of shapes on a surface. Wittgenstein calls being spatial (or again being coloured) a 'form', and expresses the point by saying that a picture can depict anything whose form it shares: the spatial picture can depict the spatial, the coloured picture anything coloured, etc.

By analogy with this conception he erects one of 'logical form'. As children we sometimes amuse ourselves by drawing imaginary maps. Given the method of projection a person could say what the imaginary country's coasts would be like. But that is not to say that the imaginary map is already a true or false map of any actual coastline. But we might say it becomes a true or false map of the world—given the method of projection—the moment we pin it to any actual place by correlating some of its points with places on the globe.

This is to suppose that we call it a true map if, correlating one point on the drawn coastline with one point on the globe, and another with another, the projection of the drawn coastline coincides with an actually existent coastline; and otherwise we call it a false map of that part of the globe. These facts, however, do not imply that, supposing it to be a false map in the sense I have defined, there is another method of projection for that map which will make it a true map of a coastline, the same points on the map and on the globe being correlated. After all, the originally selected points might be in the middle of a great ocean, in which case no method of projection would make the imaginary map a true map of a coastline.

Thus we can consider the T and F poles of the picture-proposition as giving two senses, positive and negative (as it were, the different methods of projection), in which the picture-proposition can be thought. Now although a map is a picture-proposition once a method of projection and correlations have been established, it is not so simply in virtue of its *spatial* form. For saying 'It's *not* like this' is using the map to say something true; but it is not giving a correct *map*. If then the positive and negative senses are compared to different methods of projection, then it is not the spatial form, but something comparable to spatial form, that makes the map into a picture-proposition when correlations are established. This Wittgenstein calls 'logical form'.

It is obvious enough that a proposition divides up into parts. It is also obvious that the division is not arbitrary. You cannot divide 'The cat is often drunk' into 'The cat is of' and 'ten drunk', although each part could be significant: as Wittgenstein would say, the first expression's standing to the left of the second is not what signifies in our sentence, and (3.314) 'An expression has reference only in the context of a proposition'. (It was of course on this pronouncement, and on that of Frege, repeated by Wittgenstein, that 'A name has reference only in the context of a proposition' that I modelled my statement about pictures: 'It is only in the connections that make up the picture that its elements stand for objects.')

Propositions thus have a feature that is very comparable to a feature of pictures. We call the possibility of the kind of connection that sets up a proposition 'logical form', as the possibility of any particular spatial arrangement can be called spatial form. And since logical form is that through which a structure can have T and F poles, and for something to be true or false is the very same thing as for reality to be thus or otherwise, Wittgenstein calls 'logical form' also 'the form of reality'. Thus he provides a distinctive new solution to the old old problem of shewing the connection between thought and reality. That the logical form is common to reality and the propositions is a further analogue to the way the spatial form is common to the spatial object and its spatial picture: 'A picture can depict any object whose form it has.'

The notion of logical form leads straight to that of logical space. We can construct a spatial illustration a bit like Wittgenstein's black spot on white paper, but one which 'goes lame' at a different point. If you consider an island marked on the surface of a sphere, it is clear that it defines not merely its own shape but the shape of the rest of the surface. A proposition is to be compared to such an island, its negation to the rest of the surface.

Let us say that you illustrate the concept of truth by painting the island white and the rest of the surface black, to correspond to calling a proposition true and its negation false; if on the other hand it is the negation that is true, the island is black and the rest of the surface white. Obviously you could do this with a real globe; and *any* map, real or imaginary, would divide the globe. Only as we saw, the divisions would not necessarily correspond to any actual coastlines. But the division made by the two senses of any proposition is a division of truth from falsehood; each coastline partitions the whole earth's surface, so each proposition 'reaches through the whole of the logical space'. But it *is* a proposition precisely by making a division of true from false. Now let us represent the proposition saying that *either* this *or* that is true, by a new globe with *both* the corresponding areas white; what corresponds to saying that either a proposition or its negation is true is painting the *whole* surface of the globe white—in which case you have no map. And similarly for painting the whole surface black, which would correspond to 'not (p or not p)'. But it is clear than an all-white or all-black globe is not a map.

So when—as sometimes happens in old-fashioned philosophical textbooks—the laws of contradiction and excluded middle are laid down as truth with which reason starts, this my be compared to the admiration of the sailors for the Bellman's map in the *Hunting of the Snark*:

> 'Other maps are such shapes, with their islands and capes!
> But we've got our brave captain to thank'
> (So the crew would protest) 'that he's bought us the best—
> A perfect and absolute blank!'

At 4.463 Wittgenstein uses a similar but double analogy. He says that the proposition in the positive sense is like the space in which a body can be placed; in the negative sense it is like a solid body which prevents any body from being placed in the space it occupies. Now since any proposition p divides the whole space, then the positive proposition 'p or not p' leaves the whole space empty, both the island indicated by p and the rest of the space; and its negative 'not (p or not p)' blocks the whole space.

The point at which such analogies go lame is that e.g. a globe shewing Australia as land and the rest as sea, and one shewing the rest as land and what is now Australia as sea, have the shape of a coastline in common; so that one *is* saying something about the globe if one says that either this or that representation of it is true.

On the other hand, each of these two globes could be used to depict what the other depicts, by changing the conventions for shewing sea and land. This feature does illustrate what holds for propositions: 'p' could be used to say what '∼p' says and *vice versa.* A code by which one always meant the negative of what one said need not break down. Hence, Wittgenstein says, 'though "p" and "∼p" have opposite senses, one and the same reality corresponds to them' (4.0621): the reality is the coastline itself. It is important to remember that if 'p' and 'not p' were so substituted for one another, 'not' would still mean 'not': and this is enough to shew that 'not' itself has nothing corresponding to it in reality: its presence does not determine the sense of the proposition.

We can now understand some of what Wittgenstein says about tautology and contradiction. They are not 'pictures' (4.462), just as all-white or all-black globes are not maps. And so they are not 'logical connections of signs' (4.466): the relations between them are non-significant—i.e. depict nothing: the representing relations, like two projections which between them fill a space, cancel one another out.

The all-white globe, though, might be said to be a representation of the whole world. It is because of the shape of the whole that the two shapes, p together with not-p, combine to make the shape of the whole. And this throws light on what Wittgenstein means when he says that the logical propositions describe, or rather represent, the framework of the world. 'It must shew something, that certain combinations of symbols are tautologies.' But what is represented here is not something that '*we* express by means of the signs', but that 'speaks out on its own account' (6.124).

It seems sure that the *Tractatus* account is wrong. This is partly because one cannot believe in the simple objects required by the theory; partly because it leads to dogmatic and plainly false conclusions about the will, about modality and about generalizations in infinite cases. But it is a powerful and beautiful theory: and there is surely something right about it—if one could dispense with 'simples' and draw the limits of its applicability.

It represents a high point of development of an historic line of thought. The idea that the proposition is an interweaving of simple names representing an interweaving of simple elements is to be found in Plato's *Theaetetus*; Aristotle thought about it a great deal, and rejected it largely because something more than the elements was required, something connecting them. And the idea that the complexity of a proposition reflects a complexity in its object has everywhere been influential: it is part of what is expressed, for example, in the idea of natural theologians that God, being 'simple', is not really describable or knowable—however many propositions they might construct about him.

Here it is worth remarking that the truth of the *Tractatus* theory would be death to natural theology; not because of any jejune positivism or any 'verificationism', but simply because of the picture theory of the 'significant proposition'. For it is essential to this that the picturing proposition has two poles, and in each sense it represents what may perfectly well be true. Which of them is true is just what *happens* to be the case. But in natural theology this is an impermissible notion; its propositions are not supposed to be the ones that happen to be true out of pairs of possibilities; nor are they supposed to be logical or mathematical propositions either.

Wittgenstein used to say that the *Tractatus* was not *all* wrong: it was not like a bag of junk professing to be a clock, but like a clock that did not tell you the right time. It is noticeable that he sounds like himself in the *Tractatus* whenever he writes about negation in the *Philosophical Investigations*. And at one place the voice of the author of the *Tractatus* is heard, like that of the drowned ghost in the song: 'A description is a projection of a distribution in a space.'[1]

[1] *Philosophical Investigations*, p. 187.

5

CONSEQUENCES OF THE PICTURE THEORY

Convinced that he had penetrated the essential nature of truth, falsehood and negation with his picture theory, Wittgenstein now had a great programme to carry out. He had to shew how the vast number of propositions that do not immediately appear to fit in with his theory do in fact fit in with it. There was a residue that would never fit in with it; these he dismissed as nonsensical: perhaps simply nonsensical, perhaps attempts to say the inexpressible. The following list gives us some idea of the greatness of the task. He had to deal with:

Laws of inference, and, generally, logical truths.

Statements that one proposition implies another.

Generality—i.e. propositions containing 'all' and 'some'.

Propositions giving logical classifications of terms and expressions—e.g. ' "to the right of" is a relation', ' "a is to the right of b" is a proposition'.

Propositions that are important in the foundation of mathematics such as 'a is the successor of b'.

Statements about the possibility, impossibility, necessity, and certainty of particular states of affairs.

Statements of identity.

Propositions apparently expressing functions of propositions, such as 'it is good that p', or 'p is possible', 'p is necessary' or again 'A believes p' or 'A conceives p'; and perhaps even statements about e.g. the beauty of pictures.

Propositions stating probabilities.

Propositions of mathematics.

Propositions stating laws of nature.
Propositions about space and time.
Egocentric propositions.
Propositions about the world as a whole, about God and the meaning of life.[1]

It would be wrong to suggest that Wittgenstein formed his views on all these topics simply so as to fit in with the picture-theory. It was rather in most cases that his views on them all did fit in with the picture-theory; the fact that what seemed to him true views on them did so fit in would seem an extra confirmation of the picture theory.

There is, however, one exception to this; his view, expressed at 6.37, that 'there is only *logical* necessity', and at 5.525, that the possibility of a state of affairs is simply expressed by an expression's being a significant proposition, appears to be a pure exigency of the picture theory of the proposition. It is a very common dogma at the present day that there is no sense of 'necessity' and 'possibility' except 'logical necessity' and 'logical possibility'. It is possible that this dogma, which is in part an effect of the influence of Hume, is also a hangover from the time of the overwhelming influence of the *Tractatus*.

With this is connected Wittgenstein's inference from the fact that there is no logical connection between the will and the world (6.374) (since what I intend does not *have* to come about), to the view that 'the world is independent of my will' (6.373): the connection *must* be a purely accidental one. This means that 'all happening and being this way or that', and 'everything that is the case' is independent of my will. If one should object to this that it is obvious that what people intend has some bearing on what happens, he would reply that that is just 'a phenomenon, only of interest to psychology' (6.423).

Even here, though, the view has a connection with his ideas about ethics. For the will as it appears in the world, the 'mere phenomenon, only of interest to psychology', is what is spoken of at 5.631: 'If I were to write a book: "The world as I found it", I should also have

[1] I am not able to discuss Wittgenstein's treatment of all of these topics in the compass of this book.

to give an account of my body in it, and to say which members are subject to my will and which not.' Now that such-and-such members are subject to my will is a *mere* fact; if I were suddenly so paralysed that nothing happened, the will would remain—I should still have willed; but this will is not merely an impotent thought of the thing's happening, but is of good or evil; and that, apart from the mere vulgar facts of what *happens*, is the interest of the will. But of that 'we cannot speak' because value lies outside the world and we can only express what is *in* the world. Now that value lies outside the world is not a mere consequence of Wittgenstein's picture theory of language; had he only been concerned with the fact that 'good' and 'evil' could not fit into the picture theory, he might have done as many positivists did, and debunked value altogether.

Thus the part of his views which seems to be nothing but a dogmatic consequence of the 'picture theory' is in fact his rejection of modality. Any sense of 'may', 'can', 'possible', other than that of '*logically* possible', would be unamenable to explanation in terms of the picture theory. And the assertion that something is logically possible itself requires explanation. For the picture theory does not permit any functions of propositions other than truth-functions. Indeed, we should not regard Wittgenstein's theory of the proposition as a *synthesis* of a picture theory and the theory of truth-functions; his picture theory and theory of truth-functions are one and the same. Every genuine proposition picks out certain existences and non-existences of states of affairs, as a range within which the actual existences and non-existences of states of affairs are to fall. Something with the appearance of a proposition, but which does not do this, cannot really be saying anything: it is *not* a description of any reality.

Possibility of a state of affairs is said at 5.525 to be expressed not in a proposition ('p is possible' is not a picture of a state of affairs) but in an expression's being a significant proposition: thus the logical possibility of p is one of those things that cannot be asserted, according to the *Tractatus*, but that 'shew'. This explanation does not get us much further forward. For an expression's being a significant proposition cannot be a 'fact' either: at 5.5351 we find Wittgenstein criticizing Russell for trying to symbolize the 'nonsense' ' "p" is a proposition' by the senseless tautology 'p⊃p' so as to guarantee that only propositions should be put in the argument-places of the succeeding propositions. This, he says reasonably enough, is absurd, because if that were not already assured, it could not possibly be assured by the extra premise that p⊃p, which would become not false but nonsensical with the wrong sort of substitution for 'p'.

The objection to ' "p" is a proposition' is a case of a quite general objection to a whole range of similar formations: '*n* is a number'; 'ϕ is a function'; 'it is a (possible) fact that p'; ' "the king of France" is a complex'; 'a is an object'. 'Object', 'fact', 'proposition', 'number', 'function', 'complex': all these Wittgenstein called 'formal concepts', saying (4.126): 'That anything falls under a formal concept as its object cannot be expressed by a proposition, but is shewn in the sign for the object itself. (The name shews that it designates an object, the numeral that it designates a number, etc.) Formal concepts cannot, like proper concepts, be presented by a function.' Now at least for the examples '2 is a number', 'red is a colour' the point is easily made that these propositions cannot express anything that might be false; there are not two possibilities, that 2 is, and that it is not, a number; that red is, and that it is not, a colour; of which the first happens to be actual in each case.

Carnap strongly objected to Wittgenstein's doctrine with its corollary of the 'unsayables' that are 'shewn', which seemed to lead on to the 'mysticism' of the *Tractatus*.[1] In order to avoid it, he proposed to use the 'formal mode of speech'; instead of saying 'red is a property', '2 is a number', '*to the right of* is a relation' we are to say ' "red" is a predicate', ' "2" is a numeral', ' "to the right of" is a relational expression', which were held not to involve the same difficulties.

This (perhaps deliberately) failed to take account of Wittgenstein's doctrine that the real symbol is what is common to all the symbols that can do the same job. To say of the 'real symbol' for 'to the right of'—the common feature that enables all expressions for this in all languages to have this meaning—that *it* is a relational

[1] I once had occasion to remark to Wittgenstein that he was supposed to have a mystical streak. 'Like a yellow streak,' he replied; and that is pretty well how the Vienna Circle felt about certain things in the *Tractatus*.

expression is *not* to say something that has the true-false poles. It is clear that Wittgenstein's objection to propositions in which an object is said to fall under a formal concept is not limited to the ones like 'red is a property' which are in the 'material mode of speech', and so would not be removed by translation into the 'formal mode'. 'Predicate' would be just as much a 'formal concept' for him as 'property'.

Carnap was well aware of this, and flatly denied that there was any difficulty about propositions in which an object was stated to fall under a formal concept, so long as these propositions were translated into the formal mode. At first sight this seems reasonable enough. In ' "red" is a predicate' we are saying something about the object named by the first word of the sentence; that object is itself a word. What is said about it might not have been true: the sentence therefore has the true-false poles, and Wittgenstein's supposed difficulties about it are illusory.

It is an essential part of Carnap's view that the convention of forming the name of a word by writing it in quotes is *wholly* arbitrary; there is no necessity for *any* systematic relation, any more than the names of shapes like 'square' and 'round' need have shapes corresponding to the shapes named; and 'red' *as a word* no more occurs in its name ' "red" ' than it does in 'predatory'.

Carnap's view is, however, radically defective. This was made clear by a Czech logician, K. Reach.[1] He gives a table, of which I reproduce a part here:

;	Semicolon	Secol
Semicolon	Secol	Sco

remarking that really, instead of 'table' one should say 'museum', for a table correlates names of things, whereas in a museum things and

[1] *Journal of Symbolic Logic*, September 1938: 'The Name Relation and the Logical Antinomies.'

their names are exhibited together. The table consists of two rows. In the upper row there are samples of various single symbols of a language; beneath each is a word arbitrarily chosen as a name of the given symbol. Carnap calls such a correlation of simple symbols with their arbitrary names a '*syntaktische Zuordnung*'. When we say 'red' is a colour-word, our first word is the name of an object (as it so happens, of a word); but there is no essential connection between this object and its name, other than that this *is* its name, any more than there is any other connection between, say, a man and his name; and so we may (as here) use as names of symbols, symbols that have no systematic connection with them.

Reach demonstrates the defects of Carnap's *syntaktische Zuordnung* by taking it quite seriously, as follows: 'The purpose of the sentence "Secol is the name of Semicolon" is to give information about the meaning of Secol (i.e. [the word] "Semicolon"). Does this sentence serve its purpose? Suppose somebody asks "What is the meaning of Secol?" and he receives the answer "Secol is the name of Semicolon." If the answer is to convey anything to the questioner, it must be understood; i.e. the questioner must know what Sco and Secol [i.e. what the words "Secol" and "Semicolon"] stand for in the sentence. That he knows the former [knows what Sco, i.e. the word "Secol", stands for] is shewn by the *form* of his question; but the *meaning* of his question is that he does not know the latter [he does not know what the word "Semicolon", i.e. Secol, stands for]. Hence the answer is incomprehensible to the questioner.'

Reach's work suggests the formulation of a very simple paradox, which takes Carnap's view of the use of quotation marks seriously: It is impossible to be told anyone's name by being told 'That man's name is "Smith" '; for then his name is named, not used as a name, in that statement, and so what I hear is the name of his name and not his name; and I can only learn his name if I know what name this name-of-a-name is a name of, just as I can only obey the order 'Fetch a red one' if I know what colour the colour-word 'red' is a name of. But from Reach's argument it is clear that I cannot *informatively* be told that this name-of-a-name, i.e. ' "Smith" ', is the name of the name 'Smith'; if I do not already understand this, I shall not understand the statement that it is so. This, then, seems to be a rather clear case of 'what can be shewn' but 'cannot be [informatively] said'.

Nevertheless, 'what shews' in this sense can be *illuminatingly* said. We have an (admittedly rather trivial) example of a proposition lacking the true-false poles in ' "Someone" is not the name of someone'. This is obviously true. But it does not have the bipolarity of Wittgenstein's 'significant propositions'. For what is it that it denies to be the case? Evidently, that 'someone' is the name of someone. But what would it be for 'someone' to be the name of someone? Someone might christen his child 'Someone'. But when we say ' "Someone" is not the name of someone', we are not intending to deny that anyone in the world has the odd name 'Someone'.

What then are we intending to deny? Only a piece of confusion. But this *sort* of denial may well need emphasizing. Students, for example, may believe what Professor Flew tells us in the Introduction to his collection *Logic and Language*, 1st Series, pp. 7–8: namely that 'somebody' refers to a person, that it is part of the 'logic' of 'somebody', unlike 'nobody', to refer to somebody. If this were so, then on being told that everybody hates somebody, we could ask to be introduced to this universally hated person. When we say ' "Somebody" does not refer to somebody', what we are intending to deny is what Professor Flew meant. But he did not really mean anything (even if he felt as if he did).

Here a statement which appears quite correct is not a statement with true-false poles. Its contradictory, when examined, peters out into nothingness. We may infer from this that Wittgenstein's account of propositions is inadequate, correct only within a restricted area. For it hardly seems reasonable to prohibit the formula: ' "Somebody" does not refer to somebody' or ' "Someone" is not the name of someone'; nor, of course, is this logical truth in any sharp sense of 'logical truth'. It is, rather, an insight; the opposite of it is only confusion and muddle (not contradiction).

The example of ' "Someone" is not the name of someone' is particularly clear, because the true proposition is negative. According to Wittgenstein, however, since what our proposition denies does not turn out to be anything, it itself is *not* a truth; for there isn't anything which it says is not the case, as opposed to the equally possible situation of its being the case. Therefore Wittgenstein would either have looked for a more acceptable formulation (which I think is impossible) or have said it was something which *shewed*—stared you in the face, at any rate once you had taken a good look—but could not be *said*. This partly accounts for the comical frequency with which, in expounding the *Tractatus*, one is tempted to say things and then say that they cannot be said.

At 4.1121 Wittgenstein says: 'Does not my study of sign-language correspond to the study of thought processes which philosophers have held to be so essential to the philosophy of logic? Only they got involved for the most part in inessential psychological investigations, and there is an analogous danger with my method.' The development represented by Carnap and his school seems to be a fulfilment of this expectation.

6

SIGN AND SYMBOL

As we have seen, if the possibility of a state of affairs is expressed, not in a proposition, but in an expression's being a significant proposition, then according to the *Tractatus* the very thing that it is expressed in again cannot be expressed by a proposition. But we are not yet in the realm of the 'inexpressible' according to the *Tractatus*: for instead of speaking of an expression's being a significant proposition, we could speak of the fact that ' "p" says that p'. And we shall find out that this, taken one way, is a genuine fact. To understand this we must examine two reputedly obscure passages. The first is 5.541–5.5421:

'At first sight it appears as if there were another way [other than as a truth-argument] in which one proposition could occur in another. Especially in certain psychological forms of proposition, like "A believes that p is the case" or "A conceives p" etc.[1] Here it appears superficially as if the proposition p stood in some kind of relation to an object A. And these propositions have actually been so taken in modern theory of knowledge (Russell, Moore, etc.). It is clear, however, that "A believes that p", "A conceives p", "A says p" are of the form " 'p' says p". And here what is in question is not a correlation of a fact to an object, but a correlation between facts by means of a correlation between the objects in them. This also shews that the mind—the subject etc.—as it is conceived in the superficial psychology of the present day, is a chimera. For a composite mind would no longer be a mind.'

The statement that 'A believes that p' etc. are of the form ' "p"

[1] Russell mentions such forms of proposition (*Principia Mathematica*, 1st Edition, Vol. I, p. 8) in order to explain truth-functions by contrast.

says p' has been variously taken to mean that Wittgenstein held it was impossible to have a thought without uttering a sentence; or that he held that a person was to be analysed as a complex.

For the first interpretation I can see no reason at all. Against the second it seems to be an objection that it takes a theory that a person is a complex as Wittgenstein's *ground* for saying that 'A believes p' is of the form ' "p" says that p'. Whereas it is evident that he is arguing: You can't explain the mind as 'the judging subject' in 'A judges p', *because* 'A judges p' is of the form ' "p" says p'; so that way you will only reach a complex, and a composite mind would not be a mind. Therefore Wittgenstein's statement that 'A believes p' is of the form ' "p" says p' cannot be based on any Humean theory that a person is a complex.

'It is clear,' he says; and of course what was clear to him was that for anything to be capable of representating the fact that p, it must be as complex as the fact that p; but a thought that p, or a belief or statement that p, must be potentially a representation of the fact that p (and of course actually a representation of it, if it *is* a fact that p). It is perhaps not quite right to say that 'A judges p' is of the form ' "p" says that p'; what he should have said was that the business part of 'A judges that p', the part that relates to something's having as its content a potential representation of the fact that p, was of the form ' "p" says that p': 'A believes p' or 'conceives p' or 'says p' must mean 'There occurs in A or is produced by A something which is (capable of being) a picture of p'. We should here remember the letter to Russell in which he said he did not know what the constituents of thoughts were, but he was certain that a thought must have constituents corresponding to the words of language.

Here, then, we are given ' "p" says that p' as a possible form of proposition. If Wittgenstein has not been careless, it must fit his general account of propositions—that is, it must have true-false poles. Now if a sentence is an arrangement of words, it would seem to follow in accordance with the general principles of the *Tractatus* that a way of designating a sentence must be (or be defined by) a description of its arrangement of words; though it is a reasonable complaint for a reader to make that Wittgenstein might have been more explicit than he is on this important point. The passage which comes nearest to stating it is as well known, and has been found as obscure, as the one we have just considered. It comes at 3.1432, and runs:

' "The complex sign 'aRb' says that a stands in the relation R to b." No, not that, but rather "*That* 'a' stands in a certain relation to 'b' says *that* aRb".'

This statement is really not particularly obscure. Consider what relation the sign 'a' does actually stand in to the sign 'b' in virtue of which the whole sign so composed says that aRb. There are all sorts of possibilities. For example, if I happened to write the 'a' in blue and the 'b' in red, the question could arise whether it is in virtue of the fact that 'a', 'b', and 'R' are written side by side (the order being immaterial), with the 'a' blue and the 'b' red, that the sign so composed says that aRb. In fact, we know that even if I do this, this is not the expressive feature of the sign, though of course it might be. The expressive feature is that the 'a' stands to the left and the 'b' to the right of the 'R'; for if I reversed that, putting 'b' to the left and 'a' to the right, then, according to our present conventions, a different sense would be expressed. From this we can see how we should take ' "p" says that p'. The expression schematically represented by ' "p" ', which in a concrete case would consist of an actual proposition in quotation marks, is to be taken as a way of describing the arrangement of signs that constitutes the proposition. ' "p" says that p' thus admits of various interpretations; e.g.:

'That in "*a*Rb" "a" is written in italics and "b" in Roman says that *a*Rb'

might be the way that we *interpreted* ' "*a*Rb" says that *a*Rb'. And although it contains a true description of the propositional sign as here occurring, it is a false statement (though it could be a true one); for it is not, as it happens, this fact, but the fact that '*a*' stands to the left and 'b' to the right of 'R', that says that *a*Rb. The use of italic and Roman letters is immaterial as far as concerns the expression of a relation.

If this is the sort of thing we are to understand, then the proposition ' "p" says that p' is a genuine proposition, with true-false poles, according to the conceptions of the *Tractatus*; for its truth or falsity depends on how the propositional sign 'p' is understood to be described. Of course, in order to be false, the description has got to be of some feature of the propositional sign that *might* have been used to express p. So while some interpretation or other of ' "p" says that p' *must* be true, its exact interpretation is something that can be true or false.

If a man says—perhaps wonderingly—something of the form ' "p" says p', he need not be thinking of the interpretation of the part of his expression which is a quoted expression, but that does not matter: for as Wittgenstein says at 4.002: 'Man possesses the capacity of constructing languages in which any sense can be expressed without having an inkling what each word stands for, and how. Just as we speak without knowing how the individual sounds are produced. . . . The tacit conventions for understanding ordinary language are enormously complicated.' Someone who had given no thought to *how* '*a*Rb' says that *a*Rb would immediately know that someone else had gone wrong who thought that it was the italics that mattered, and that one could say that bR*a* by writing 'aR*b*'.

That is to say, in ' "p" says that p' what is being considered is the propositional *sign*, mental or physical; and it was of course primarily of the physical sign that Wittgenstein was thinking. Signs are after all what we actually hear or see; it is from them that we gather the meaning of what is said or written; and *some* of the variations in them embody variations of meaning. That is to say, the kind of sensibly perceived difference that there is between 'aRb' and 'bRa' is that from which we gather, and by means of which we express, *a* difference of sense.

Now if we consider the difference between

A and B are poetical

and

A and B are identical

we shall have gone far wrong if we think that the difference in sense between the two propositions is expressed purely by the difference of four letters, that in the one one thing is asserted of A and B, and in the other another thing, the difference of words expressing a difference just in *what* is asserted. For that difference of two words signifies much more than that; as comes out in the fact that if A and B are poetical, A is poetical; whereas if A and B are identical, we can't go on from this to say 'A is identical'. Thus Wittgenstein says: 'What does not get expressed in the signs, comes out in their application: What the signs fail to express, their application declares.' By 'application' he did not mean 'role in life', 'use', 'practice of the use' in the sense of *Philosophical Investigations*; he meant 'logico-syntactic application' (i.e. that kind of difference between the syntactical roles of words which concerns a logician). 'Only together with its logico-syntactic application does a sign determine a logical form' (3.327). And it was by the possession of a logical form that a proposition was capable of expressing a sense.

But it is pretty well impossible to discern logical form in everyday language. As an example of the difficulty, consider the difference between Roman and Arabic numeration. MCMXLVIII is the same number as 1948, but reading it is more complicated. For example, the way of reading MCM is different from the way of reading VII, though each is composed of three of the elements placed side by side. This does not mean that the Roman system fails to express the same number as the Arabic. It expresses it perfectly.

This illustrates Wittgenstein's view of the difference between ordinary language and a good symbolic notation. In his Introduction (p. 9) Russell said that Wittgenstein was 'concerned with the conditions for a logically perfect language—not that any language is logically perfect, or that we believe ourselves capable, here and now, of constructing a logically perfect language, but that the whole function of language is to have meaning, and it only fulfils this function in proportion as it approaches to the ideal language which we postulate.' This statement of Russell's was plainly contrary to the intentions of the *Tractatus*, as is very easily shewn. At 5.5563 Wittgenstein says: 'All the sentences of our everyday language, just as they are, are logically in perfect order.' Language could not *approximate* to having meaning; any language, just *qua* language, fulfils its purpose perfectly.

It is a mistake to suppose that the dictum 'Ordinary language is all right' is an expression only of Wittgenstein's later views. He was dialectically expounding, not opposing, his point of view at the time of writing the *Tractatus*, in the following passage of *Philosophical Investigations*:

> 'On the one hand it is clear that every sentence in our language "is all right as it is". That is, that we are not *striving* after an ideal: as if our ordinary vague sentences had not yet got an irreproachable sense, and a perfect language had yet to be constructed by us. On the other hand this seems clear: Where there is sense, there must be perfect order. And so there must be perfect order even in the vaguest sentence.'[1]

That is to say, the sentences of ordinary language no more fail to express a sense than our Roman numeral fails to express a number. The one expresses a sense, the other a number, perfectly. And so the ideal order that characterizes language is there in every sentence of ordinary language. But: 'Everyday language is a part of the human organism and is just as complicated. It is humanly impossible to gather the logic of language from it directly' (4.002). This, then, is why, according to Wittgenstein, we study logic and construct logical symbolisms: in order to understand the 'logic of language', so as to see how language mirrors reality.

We want in pursuit of the picture-theory to be able to say that the expressive feature of language is that *signs* are *combined in certain ways*. We compared 'aRb', and 'bRa', saying that we have here a sensible difference in which a difference of sense is expressed. That is to say, this is a particular instance of a *kind* of difference which is essential to *any* relational expression in any language: we have here an example of 'what is common to all symbols that can do the job'. But of course 'aRb' expresses something, as e.g. 'X-O' does not, because the elements in 'aRb' are not just *signs* in the sense of 'marks', but are *symbols*, as those in 'X-O' are not. So the expressive feature of 'aRb' is not just an order of elements, but is the fact that a *sign* 'a', which is a *symbol*, stands to the left, and the *sign* 'b', which is also a symbol, to the right, of the *sign*—again a symbol—'R'.

[1] *Pnilosophical Investigations*, Part I, §95.

On the other hand, we have to remember the central point of the picture theory which we have already explained: 'Only in the context of a proposition has a name reference'; 'Only in the context of a proposition has an expression reference.' This prohibits us from thinking that we can *first* somehow characterize 'a', 'R' and 'b' as symbolic signs, and *then* lay it down how we can build propositions out of them. If 'a' is a symbolic sign only in the context of a proposition, then the symbol 'a' will be properly presented, not by putting it down and saying it is a symbol of such and such a kind, but by representing the whole class of the propositions in which it can occur.

This we may do provisionally by taking a proposition in which 'a' occurs, and retaining 'a', while we substitute a variable (I will use 'ξ') for all the rest of the proposition. Then the symbol 'a' is rightly presented, not just by putting it down and saying it is a sign of an object, but by a variable proposition

$$(\xi)\mathrm{a}$$

This Wittgenstein says quite generally for symbols, or 'expressions', at 3.311–3.313: 'The expression presupposes the forms of all propositions in which it can occur. It is the common characteristic mark of a class of propositions. It is therefore presented by the general form of the propositions of which it is characteristic. And in this form the expression will be *constant* and everything else *variable*. Thus the expression is presented by a variable: the propositions which contain the expressions are values of this variable.... I call such a variable a "propositional variable".' Equally, of course, it would have been possible, considering a proposition such as 'aRb' in which 'a' occurs, to take 'Rb' as the expression to be presented, and to substitute a variable (I will use 'η') for the 'a'; then the expression will be presented by the variable proposition

$$(\eta)\mathrm{Rb}$$

This account is perhaps inspired by Frege's *Concept and Object*. Frege said:

'Language has means of presenting now one, now another part of the sentence as the subject; one of the most familiar is the distinction of active and passive forms. . . . It need not then surprise us that the same sentence may be conceived as an assertion about a concept and also as an assertion about an object; only we must observe that what is asserted is different.'[1]

Frege was thinking at first of the fact that we can re-form propositions, as is shewn by his reference to active and passive forms. Language shews now one, now another, part of the sentence as the subject, by altering the sentence, so that now one part, now another, appears as the grammatical subject. e.g. 'John murdered James', 'James was murdered by John'. And, also, 'The sun is red', 'Red is a property of the sun'.

But when Frege says: 'The same sentence can be conceived as an assertion about a concept and also about an object; only we must observe that what is asserted is different', he has passed from considering a reformulation of 'The sun is red', like 'Redness is a property of the sun', to considering the one sentence 'The sun is red' in two ways. And these two ways are very well explained by Wittgenstein. Adopting his explanations we can take them as the alternatives of regarding it as a value of a variable sentence:

'– – – – – – red'

which takes 'The sun' as an argument, and

'The sun – – – – – –'

which takes 'red' as argument. In the first, we shall therefore be regarding the sentence as 'about' the sun; in the second as 'about' red—for what we are 'taking as the subject' is what fills the argument-place. Only, as Frege says, if we so regard the sentence as now an assertion about a concept, now about an object, what is asserted is different, though the sense of the whole analysis is in each case the same.

[1] *Philosophical Writings of Gottlob Frege*, ed. Geach and Black, p. 49.

This last point was missed by Ramsey in his essay *Universals*. He speaks of a theory—which he rejects—that in a proposition 'aRb' we can discern 'three closely related propositions; one asserts that the relation R holds between the terms a and b, the second asserts the possession by a of the complex property of "having R to b", while the third asserts that b has the complex property that a has R to it. These must be three different propositions because they have three different sets of constituents, and yet they are not three propositions, but one proposition, for they all say the same thing, namely that a has R to b. So the theory of complex universals is responsible for an incomprehensible trinity. . . .' Ramsey's thought is bedevilled at this point by the idea that you cannot analyse a proposition in a variety of ways: that if you say that 'Socrates taught Plato' ascribes something to Socrates, you cannot also say that it ascribes something to Plato without making it out a different proposition.

Ramsey's essay, however, quite apart from its intrinsic interest, is also very helpful for exegesis of the *Tractatus* theory of 'expressions'. For Wittgenstein tells us at 3.314 that every variable can be conceived as a propositional variable—even the variable name. But how can this be? The variable proposition

x loves Socrates

has as values only those propositions in which a name is substituted for x; but the propositional variable

ξ loves Socrates

indicated by Wittgenstein has as values *all* the propositions in which 'loves Socrates' occurs, e.g. 'Everyone loves Socrates', 'Anyone who loves Plato loves Socrates', 'No one loves Socrates', 'Plato does not love Socrates'. And similarly for all other variables, as variables are usually understood. 'Plato has n sons' is a variable proposition whose values are e.g. 'Plato has 6 sons', 'Plato has 100 sons', 'Plato has no sons', but not 'Plato has stupid sons', or 'Plato has as good sons as Socrates'. That is to say, its values are *not* all the propositions in which the expression 'Plato has . . . . sons' can occur.

Here, following Ramsey, we may draw a distinction between a wider and a narrower range of propositions which an expression can be used to collect. Only there is no need to follow Ramsey in holding that the expression 'Socrates' cannot be used to collect a range including e.g. 'Socrates is wise and Plato is not'. For this opinion of Ramsey's was based on his rejection of 'complex universals'; and this in turn is based on his conviction that if you define e.g. 'ϕx' as 'aRx', and then treat 'ϕ' as a predicate of b in 'ϕb', you must be denying that 'ϕb' is a relational proposition—which of course is absurd, if you have defined 'ϕx' as 'aRx'.

Now it may be that proponents of 'complex universals' were confutable by this argument; but it does not follow that anyone who, like Frege, picks a name out of a proposition and calls the rest of the proposition a predicate can be dealt with in this way. Only Ramsey's belief that one analysis of a proposition excludes all others enabled him, just on the strength of this argument, to deny that 'Socrates' could be used to collect just as varied a range of propositions as e.g. 'wise'. For he thinks that 'wise' *can* be used to collect such propositions as e.g. 'Neither Socrates nor Plato is wise' or 'Someone is wise'. And he goes on to distinguish between a wider and a narrower range of such propositions: one, *all* the propositions in which 'wise' occurs, and the other a narrower collection of simpler propositions, of the form 'x is wise'. We can adopt this distinction, just as he intends it for 'wise', for 'Socrates' also.

Now the question arises: why is there no hint of this in Wittgenstein's text? It would certainly seem from what Wittgenstein says that the 'class of propositions' of which an expression was 'the common characteristic mark' was the *whole* class of propositions in which the expression could occur. But 'x loves Socrates' can only be completed into a proposition by substituting a *name* for 'x'; therefore 'x loves Socrates' *cannot* give us the general form of the whole class of propositions, in which the expression 'loves Socrates' occurs. We seem to be forced to call Ramsey's distinction to our aid, and say that the 'class of propositions' presented by 'x loves Socrates' is a narrower class that can be discerned within the wider class of all the propositions in which 'loves Socrates' can occur.

The answer to this puzzle lies in the theory—which is integral to the picture theory of the proposition—that all propositions are truth-functions of the elementary propositions.[1] On this theory, the 'wider class' that we have been considering will be the class of all the truth-functions of any set of propositions among which are propositions containing the expression in question. It immediately follows from this that any expression presupposes the most general form of all propositions, as well as the special form of the proposition in which it immediately occurs. But unless—which is very possible—I have missed some essential feature of Wittgenstein's idea,[2] it must be admitted that his account is sketchy, unsatisfactory and obscure.

[1] In particular, general propositions such as 'Everyone loves Socrates'. *See* Chapter 11.

[2] It is possible that Wittgenstein was satisfied with 'the great works of Frege' as far as concerns the general form of all propositions in which a given predicate (such as 'loves Socrates' or 'is clever') occurs. Frege's general form is '$M_{\beta}\phi(\beta)$': this is the general form of second-level functions, such as 'Everything is ϕ', 'Something is ϕ', 'ϕ is what James is and John is not'. The 'β' shews that ϕ is a concept or first-level function, being the mark of an argument-place.

7

WITTGENSTEIN, FREGE AND RAMSEY

We have inferred from Wittgenstein's remarks on 'expressions'—which must include names—that a name 'a' can be represented by a propositional variable '(ξ)a' which is an informal—and somewhat uninformative—version of the most general form of propositions in which 'a' occurs. Thus Wittgenstein would not accept Frege's way of distinguishing between object and concept—that an object is something complete in itself, whereas a concept is in need of completion—is, as it were, something with a hole in it. For it looks as if Wittgenstein will make out both that expression in a sentence which designates an object, and that expression which remains over in the sentence when we have picked out the expression designating the object, to be something with, so to speak, a hole in it. And this conception is the same as the picture theory, in terms of which we have explained what Wittgenstein meant by Frege's dictum: 'Only in the context of the proposition has a name reference.'

Ramsey, in his essay on 'Universals', took Wittgenstein to mean that there was no difference between qualities and objects.

> 'Against Mr. Russell it might be asked how there can be such objects as his universals, which contain the form of a proposition and are incomplete. In a sense, it might be urged, all objects are incomplete; they cannot occur in facts except in conjunction with other objects, and they contain the form of propositions of which they are constituents. In what way do universals do this more than anything else?'

Ramsey therefore suggests that it is mere prejudice to distinguish between individuals and qualities; there is no reason why we should not speak of Socrates' attaching to ϕ as well as of ϕ's attaching to Socrates in a proposition 'ϕ Socrates'.

The distinction has a practical point, he says, in that if 'ϕ' stands for e.g. 'either having R to a or having S to b', we cannot put $\phi =$ Ra v Sb because we should not know whether the blanks in ( )Ra and ( )Sb were to be filled with the same or different arguments. Instead we must put ϕx=xRa v xSb; which explains not what is meant by ϕ by itself, but that followed by any symbol x it is short for 'xRa v xSb'. But if ϕ were a simple property, there would be no reason to say that 'ϕ' is asserted of Socrates rather than that 'Socrates' is asserted of the reference of 'ϕ'. And he takes this to be Wittgenstein's doctrine, chiefly because he observed quite correctly that Wittgenstein holds that both a name, and the remainder of a sentence from which a name has been removed, are represented by 'propositional variables'; moreover, Wittgenstein does not speak of 'concepts' or 'universals' as a kind of thing that is to be found in the world: it is quite clear that for him there is nothing but objects in configuration.

That Ramsey has mistaken Wittgenstein's intention is fairly clear from Wittgenstein's calling 'function', like 'object', a formal concept (*see* Chapter 9) and from his explanation at 4.24: 'Names are simple symbols, I indicate them by single letters ("x", "y", "z"). The elementary proposition I write as a function of names in the form "f(x)", "ϕ(x,y)".' Now it must not be supposed from this that Wittgenstein intends 'ϕ(x,y)' to represent an atomic fact consisting of three objects. He has only just remarked (4.2211): 'Even if the world is infinitely complex, so that every fact consists of infinitely many atomic facts and every atomic fact is composed of infinitely many objects, even so there must be objects and atomic facts.' So when he writes 'ϕ(x,y)', nothing whatever is indicated about how many names may be covered by the sign of the function; there might, on the hypothesis that he has just mentioned, be an infinite number.

Wittgenstein's doctrine, however, is not at all easy to understand; for on the one hand he speaks of the elementary proposition as a concatenation of names, as consisting of names in immediate combination; and on the other hand he says at 5.47: 'Where there is complexity, there is argument and function': therefore the elementary proposition too consists of argument and function.

These remarks considered together raise the problem: if the elementary proposition consists of names in immediate connection—if it is just a concatenation of names—then it is not *reproduced*, even if it can be faithfully represented, by a formula consisting of some letters for names and some letters for functions. And this is borne out by many passages. Notably for example 3.143: 'The nature of the propositional sign becomes very clear, if we imagine it as composed of three-dimensional objects (say tables, chairs, books) instead of written signs. Here the spatial lay-out of those things expresses the sense of the proposition.' We are reminded of the models of cars, buses and buildings set out in a law court to shew how an accident took place, which made Wittgenstein say: 'That's what a proposition is!' And in the succeeding entry, which we have already considered, he says: 'That "a" stands in a certain relation toi "b" says *that* aRb.' Now the actual relation in which, in the propositonal sign 'aRb' 'a' stands to 'b' was, as we remarked, that 'a' stands to the left, and 'b' to the right, of a further sign 'R'. Now let 'R' be 'to the left of'. In a waxwork display shewing the way people stood, the fact that a man A stood to the left of a man B will be shewn by having the wax figure that goes proxy for A in the display standing to the left of the wax figure that goes proxy for B, and there will be no need for any third object to signify the relation. At 4.0311 Wittgenstein makes the comparison with the *tableau vivant*: 'One name stands for one thing, another for another, they are connected together: that is how the whole images the atomic fact—like a *tableau vivant*.'

It is natural—and reasonable—to say of this idea: This is all very well; but it is possible only when the picture-proposition shares a 'form' as Wittgenstein calls it, *other* than what he calls 'logical form', with what it depicts. The waxwork show and the *tableau vivant* need no figures going proxy for the spatial relations just because, being three-dimensional models of three-dimensional situations, they can reproduce the spatial relations instead of having something standing for them. And the coloured picture can represent that a cloak is red without having the cloak in one place and the redness in another, just because it is a coloured picture representing something coloured, so that it can simply shew the cloak as red. Further, even if the picture were in black and white, and represented the colour of objects by some conventionally agreed shading—still, it has the advantage of being able to shew the shading that means red, *on* the cloak and not somewhere else.

This is exactly what does not happen in a proposition. In a sentence saying that the man wore a red cloak the word for the cloak is not printed in red to shew this. Even if we had some such conventions—and perhaps we can admit we have something of the sort in the difference between 'aRb' and 'bRa'—they do not take us very far. Even in this very favourable case, we need a special sign for the relation itself.[1] And rightly so, because there is some material content to relations like 'to the right of' or 'bigger than'; that is why signs between which the same kind of relations hold can reproduce them; but if you were quite generally to express relations between things by relations between their signs, then you would need to have as many different relations between signs as we in practice have words to express relations.

This is in fact Wittgenstein's requirement for the fully analysed sentences of a language. For the fully analysed elementary proposition is a concatenation of simple names; though not a mere list, because the way they are combined is expressive.

This does not mean that function and argument would disappear in the final analysis. If for the moment we may give 'a-b-c-d' as an elementary proposition, then 'a-b-c-( )' and 'a-(′)-(′′)-d' would be two different functions; which might be represented as 'fx', 'ϕ(x,y)' respectively; and the representations of 'a-b-c-d' as a value of these two functions would be 'fd', 'ϕ(b,c)'. I write primes in the second function to shew that it can be completed with different names in the two empty argument-places. (′)-(′′)-(′′′)-(′′′′) would be a formula, 'a logical form—a logical proto-picture', of an elementary proposition.

Now we just do not know the composition of any elementary proposition; that is why Wittgenstein never gives any such example. But Ramsey writes as if, say, 'a-b' were a specifiable elementary

[1] A case in which no sign occurs for the relation itself is 'Caius Marci' in Latin—'Caius (is the son) of Marcus'.

proposition, which Wittgenstein *chooses* to write as, say, 'f(b)'. That is quite to misunderstand Wittgenstein's use of the sign 'f' in 'f(b)': 'f(b)' symbolizes an elementary proposition, but not necessarily one in whose sense (the atomic fact) *only* two objects occur. The point can be put most briefly like this: to represent a name 'a' by '(ξ)a', i.e. by the most general way for that name to occur in a proposition, is not to represent a name as a function, but only to stress that the name has reference only in the context of a proposition.

The idea of conceiving a proposition as a function of the expressions contained in it comes from Frege, and to understand it we have to go back to his great essay *Function and Concept* and follow the steps by which he formulated this conception.

First we introduce the notion of a numerical *function*—i.e. what is expressed by a numerical formula containing one or more 'indefinitely indicating' letters; if the letter or letters are replaced by signs for a definite number or numbers, the expression so obtained has a definite numerical value: e.g. x^2, $x+y$. The function could be fittingly expressed by a formula with an empty place in it: $(\ )^2$. By an 'argument' we mean what is signified by the sign we put into the empty place. 'We give the name "the value of a function for an argument" to the result of completing the function with the argument.' Thus e.g. 4 is the value of the function $(\ )^2$ for the argument 2. But it is necessary, if there is more than one empty place, to distinguish between cases where the function can be completed by putting different things, and cases where it must be completed by putting the same thing, into the empty places. That is why we use letters instead of empty places.

There are functions whose value is always the same, whatever the argument, such as $2+x-x$; and there are pairs of functions whose values are always the same for the same argument: for example x^2-4x and $x(x-4)$.[1]

Following Frege, we now add to the signs $+$, $-$, etc., which serve for constructing a functional expression, such signs as $=$, $>$, $<$, which occur in arithmetical statements. So we speak of the function $x^2=1$. The value of the function for a given argument is signified by the result of substituting a definite numeral for the letter

[1] I follow Frege in speaking of *two* functions here. It is not usual.

x. But the result of substituting a definite numeral for x here has not a numerical value, but is something true or false; hence the now familiar idea of a 'truth-value' is derived from this conception of Frege's.

The 'value' of $x^2=1$ is 'true' for a definite argument, e.g. for -1; to say this is the same thing as to say that -1 is a square root of 1, or that -1 has the property that its square is 1, or that -1 falls under the concept 'square root of 1'. 'We thus see,' Frege says, 'how closely what is called a concept in logic is connected with what we call a function.' This suggests an interesting definition of a proposition as 'the result of completing a sign of a function by filling up an argument-place, when the value of the result is a truth-value'. And so far, Wittgenstein is in agreement with Frege, and expresses his agreement at 3.318: 'I conceive the proposition—like Frege and Russell—as a function of the expressions it contains.'

To speak of conceiving the proposition as a function *of* the expressions it contains is of course not inconsistent with denying, as Frege does, that a proposition is a function; it is like speaking of 8 as a function of 2, say its cube. It is important to grasp this point, that what is a function *of* something is not a function *tout court*; confusion on this point is often found. A function for example is sometimes explained as a variable magnitude. Now it is true that, say, the volume of a gas is a variable magnitude (i.e. variable in time) and is also a function of the pressure and temperature. But the volume of a gas is not a function *tout court*, and therefore we do not get here an example of a function that is a variable magnitude. To say that the volume is a function of pressure and temperature is to say that there is a function f such that $V=f(p,t)$. For the volume to be a function *tout court* would be represented by the nonsense $V=f(\ )$.

We must now consider Frege's next step. He has defined a function as what is signified by an expression with an empty place; and he says: 'An object is anything that is not a function, so that the expression for it does not contain an empty place.' It follows that (unasserted) propositions designate objects, since they have no empty places; and since Frege regards a proposition as one kind of completed functional expression, and considers that a completed functional expression (e.g. '2^3') is a designation of a value of the function, it becomes natural to say that propositions designate values. This might be a matter of terminology, to which it would be unreasonable to object, granted that the conception of a proposition as a completed functional expression recommends itself.

Frege now proceeds to construct a function

——x

whose value is 'the true' when 'the true' is its argument, and in *all* other cases is the false. By taking 'the true' as argument Frege means putting a true proposition in place of the 'x'; you can put a designation of anything there instead—a false proposition or a definite description of a numeral or an ordinary proper name: anything, in short, that stands for anything, without having any empty places in it. For example

——2

is a possible result of completing this function, and the value of the function when so completed is: false, or, as Frege puts it, ——2 *is* the false. This way of speaking is of course a consequence of the distinction between sense and reference. If I use an expression which stands for something, then in using it I am speaking of what it stands for; and if I have another name, 'B', for that thing, I can use the first name, 'A', and say that A *is* B. So since '——2' is a designation of the truth-value: false, Frege can say that ——2 is the false. We must accept this sort of consequence if we accept the *prima facie* plausible distinction between the sense and reference of expressions; this constitutes an objection to the distinction.

The reason why Frege wished to construct such a function is that he has no truck with attempts to stipulate ranges of significance in the manner of Russell.[1] If a truth-value is an object, it can be an argument; but he is not willing to specify 'propositions' as the range of significant substitutions for 'x' in functions taking truth-values

[1] *See* Chapter 9, pp. 123–4.

as arguments; and indeed the specification of ranges of significance is a very dubious business.

Ordinarily, if we write down '5 >4' we wish to assert something; but according to Frege's view, '5 >4' is just an expression for a truth-value, without any assertion. Therefore, he says, we need a special sign in order to be able to assert something, as opposed to expressing *a mere assumption*[1]—the putting of a case without a

[1] It has sometimes perplexed readers of Wittgenstein that he refers, both in the *Tractatus* (4.063), and in *Philosophical Investigations*, to 'the Fregean *Annahme*', as if '*Annahme*' (assumption) had been a technical term in Frege, as it was in Meinong. His reference is to this passage; and it is evident that his attention was especially fixed on it by a passage in Russell's account of Frege in the *Principles of Mathematics*, Appendix A, §477. Russell says: 'There are, we are told, three elements in judgment: (1) the recognition of truth, (2) the *Gedanke* (the thought), (3) the truth-value. Here the *Gedanke* is what I have called an unasserted proposition—or rather, what I have called by this name covers both the *Gedanke* alone and the *Gedanke* together with its truth-value. It will be well to have names for these two distinct notions; I shall call the *Gedanke* alone a *propositional concept*; the truth-value of a *Gedanke* I shall call an *assumption*.' And here Russell has a footnote referring to the passage in *Function and Concept*, and, saying: 'Frege, like Meinong, calls this an *Annahme*'. 'Formally, at least,' he goes on, 'an assumption does not require that its content should be a propositional concept; whatever x may be, "the truth of x" is a definite notion. This means the true if x is true, and if x is false or not a proposition it means the false.'

What Russell refers to as 'the truth of x' is of course Frege's function ——x. Frege introduces a second function

—┬—x

whose value is the false for just those arguments for which the value of ——x is the true. Thus, as Russell says, we do not have assertions and negations—there is not a negation sign, corresponding to the assertion sign—but we have assertions of the truth and falsity of 'thoughts', or, as Russell calls them, 'propositional concepts'.

It is a peculiarity of Russell's account that he takes

——5 >4

to be something different from

5 >4

and calls '5 >4' the 'thought' and '——5 >4' the 'assumption'; thus turning Frege's quite innocent and untechnical expression 'a mere assumption' into a technicality.

What Russell failed to notice was that if a proposition is substituted simultaneous judgment as to whether it holds or not. So he puts a vertical stroke at the left of the horizontal, e.g.

|——2+3=5

and *this* expresses the *assertion* that 2+3=5.

We must now examine Wittgenstein's main criticism of Frege. At 4.431, he says: 'The proposition is the expression of its truth-conditions', and then remarks: 'Hence Frege was quite right to premise the truth-conditions as defining the signs of his symbolism.' The reference is presumably to the passage in the *Grundgesetze*

for x in '——x' there is no difference at all, for Frege, either in sense or in reference, between the proposition by itself and the proposition with the horizontal stroke attached; moreover a 'thought' is not a proposition, not even an unasserted proposition, but is the sense of a proposition, and hence there is the same *Gedanke* when we have a proposition and when we have a proposition with the stroke attached. It is only when we substitute the designation of something *other* than a truth-value for 'x' in '——x' that there is any difference, either in sense or in reference, between the designation by itself and the designation with the stroke attached. In that case, the designation designates whatever it does designate—the Moon or the number 3 for example; and the designation with the stroke attached designates a truth-value, in these cases the false.

Russell's remarks, which mistakenly give special prominence to Frege's use of the word 'assumption', must be the source of Wittgenstein's references to it. Further, it appears that Wittgenstein actually accepted Russell's interpretation; for his comment on Frege at the end of 4.063 is not otherwise intelligible: 'The proposition does not stand for any object (truth-value) whose properties are called "true" or "false"; the verb of the proposition is not "is true" or "is false"—as Frege thought—but what "is true" must already contain the verb.' Although in *Begriffsschrift* Frege said that the verb of the proposition was 'is true'—a view which he rejected in *Sense and Reference*—he never thought this of 'is false'. But if we were to adopt Russell's interpretation of the passage in *Function and Concept*, we should say that according to Frege there are three stages

(1) x
(2) the truth of x
or: the falsehood of x

and then (3) the final stage of assertion, which we might think of as a tick put against whichever is right, the truth of x or the falsehood of x; and *such* a view might easily be rendered as a view that the real verb in the proposition that gets asserted—i.e. in the 'assumption'—is 'is true' or 'is false'.

where Frege says that he has specified the reference, i.e. the truth-value, of any well-formed proposition in his symbolism by specifying the truth-conditions, and that the *sense* of the proposition is the sense of: such-and-such truth-conditions are fulfilled. 'Only,' Wittgenstein continues, 'the explanation of the concept of truth is wrong: if "the true" and "the false" were really objects, and were the arguments in ~p etc., then according to Frege's own specifications the sense of ~p would by no means be specified.'

Frege has specified the truth-*values* of his propositions by specifying the truth-*conditions*, because his propositions are logical truths: it is the characteristic feature of logical truths (or again of logical falsehoods) that their truth-values are determined by determining their truth-conditions. But he has also said that the sense of his propositions is the sense of this: that their truth-conditions are fulfilled; and in this way he has ensured that his propositions are scientifically perfect; he has guaranteed a sense and a reference for them, and determined which truth-value they have.

Thus, if Frege has a negative proposition, '~p', its sense must also be the sense of the fulfilment of its truth-conditions. But his explanation of negation is this: he introduces a new function —┬—x, whose value is the false for just those arguments for which the value of ——x is the true, and conversely; and so in '~p' we have a proposition determined as expressing the result of completing with the argument 'p' a function whose value for given arguments is given; but where is the *sense* of '~p'? '~p' appears to be defined in effect as that proposition whose reference is the true in certain circumstances and the false in others. But on Frege's own principles you do not specify a sense by specifying a reference; and so, Wittgenstein says, according to Frege's own principles, the sense of '~p' is not determined.[1]

The problems involved here are at bottom the same as those I discussed in Chapter 3. As a criticism of Frege the point can be summarized by saying: 'If truth-values are the references of propositions, then you do not specify a sense by specifying a truth-value.'

[1] This criticism is quite independent of the misinterpretation of Frege's theory (taken over by Wittgenstein from Russell) which was discussed in the last footnote.

Now this objection is quite decisive; but the essential difficulty about negation, although it receives a special form in connection with Frege's theory, is, as we have already seen, not generated just by Frege's conceptions. We encountered it at the very outset, when we examined the customary definition of '~p' as *the* proposition that is true when p is false and false when p is true; and we have seen how Wittgenstein's picture theory of the proposition guaranteed the legitimacy of the customary definition by supplying the conditions required for offering such a definition: namely that there is not more than one such proposition and that there always is such a proposition.

Furthermore, negation gives us good grounds for rejecting Ramsey's suggestions, not just as interpretations of the *Tractatus*, but in themselves. For you can negate a function, but not an object: this shews that even the simplest possible sign of a function is not the same thing as a name. It may be asked why, in analysing 'Socrates is not wise', we should not take the negation with 'Socrates' rather than with 'wise'—'Socrates-is-not wise'. We can certainly speak of 'all the things that *Socrates is not*'; and Frege would have said that this phrase stood for a second-level concept, its role being to say, concerning the reference of a predicate, that this is one of the things Socrates is not. But though it can be treated as an 'expression', the common characteristic mark of a class of propositions, 'Socrates is not' is not on an equal footing with 'Socrates'—they cannot be treated as one another's contradictories, like 'red' and 'not red'. The result of attaching 'Socrates is not' to the conjunction of predicates 'wise and just' is quite different from the conjunction of the results of attaching it to 'wise' and 'just'; for the name 'Socrates' no such difference can arise. Accordingly, 'Socrates is not' is not an allowable interpretation of a name variable, in the way that a negative predicate is always an allowable interpretation of a predicate variable.

It should be apparent, however, that Wittgenstein's views are extremely Fregean. What, then, has become of Frege's 'concepts' in Wittgenstein's theory? They seem to have disappeared entirely; actually, however, instead of making concepts or universals into a kind of objects, as Ramsey wished to, Wittgenstein made the gulf between concepts and objects much greater than Frege ever made it. So far as concerns the content of a functional expression, that will consist in the objects covered by it. But in respect of having argument-places, concepts go over entirely into logical forms. In the 'completely analysed proposition', which is 'a logical network sprinkled with names',[1] the Fregean 'concept', the thing with holes in it, has become simply the logical form. Thus there is no question of two kinds of *reference* for expressions; one which is incomplete, having a hole in it that awaits, say, an object to complete it; and another, complete and capable of completing the incomplete, itself requiring no completion.

An interesting consequence follows about, say, two propositions expressing (completely) different facts: A is red, and: B is red. If these propositions were 'completely analysed', so that we had elementary propositions consisting of names in immediate connection, then the question arises whether the *objects* that would be named, in place of our using the colour-word 'red' in the two cases, would be different. I think Ramsey would have supposed that they would be the same. And no doubt he would have pooh-poohed the feeling that in that case these objects would have the character of universals rather than 'individuals'; we don't think A is a 'universal' because it can enter into a variety of facts, so why should we think this of red—or if red is composite, of the objects into which 'red' is 'analysed'? This is perhaps a proper reply; yet it is difficult not to feel that an object that can exist all over the world in different facts has rather the character of a universal. It takes a little mental habituation to think that existence in several facts is the only feature that counts, so that since both A and red can exist in several facts, we should not be impressed by A's at least existing in only one place at a time, while red can exist in so many.

[1] I take this expression from a late notebook of Wittgenstein's in which he makes some comments on the theories of the *Tractatus*. In his pre-*Tractatus* notebooks Wittgenstein says: 'Properties and relations are objects too' (16.6.15). On my view, he no longer holds this in the *Tractatus*. I think my view necessary (a) to reconcile the various passages I have cited about functions and elementary propositions and (b) because if Wittgenstein held that objects fell into such radically distinct categories as functions and individuals, it is an incredible omission not to have made this clear.

Anyhow, whatever the merit of Ramsey's view, he is incorrect in ascribing it to Wittgenstein. Let us pretend once more that we can make an actual model of an elementary proposition 'with the names in immediate connection'; then for Wittgenstein the two facts: A is red, and: B is red, would be analysed into (1) facts corresponding to the descriptions of the complexes A and B, and (2) facts about the elements of the complex A along with certain further elements, say a, b, c, for A's redness, and exactly corresponding facts about the elements of the complex B along with certain other elements, say d, e, f, for B's redness. There is no need for a, b, c, to be the same as d, e, f, respectively; for it is only the 'logical network' that is 'universal'.

We normally tend to assume that different occurrences (at least of the same shade) of red differ only in that there are different *things that are* red—that no real difference other than this answers to the two predications of the predicate 'red'. This has helped to form the belief in universals; though there have been philosophers, e.g. among the medievals, who have wished to speak of 'individualized forms'—'this whiteness' for example. The problem of 'universals' can in fact be given the form: was Frege right to introduce two wholly different kinds of 'reference' for words, namely 'objects' and 'concepts'? A 'concept' was the 'reference' of a predicate; now the characteristic mark of a predicate is its possession of an argument-place or -places, which could be filled with the names of now one, now another object; hence a 'concept' is a 'universal'. In Wittgenstein's fully analysed proposition, we have nothing but a set of argument-places filled with names of objects; there remains no kind of expression that could be regarded as standing for a concept.

The objects 'behind' a true predication of 'red' would indeed be of the same logical form in every case. We must remember that the original seat of form is the objects themselves: 'If things can occur in atomic facts, this must be something that is in things themselves. . . . If I can imagine an object in the nexus of an atomic fact, I cannot imagine it outside the *possibility* of this nexus.' (2.0121): And that is why Wittgenstein says: 'The possibility of its occurrence in atomic facts is the form of the object' (2.0141), and: 'The objects form the substance of the world' (2.021); and so they are '*form and content*' (2.025). Thus at 2.0231 we learn that the substance of the world—i.e. the objects—*can* determine only a form, not any material properties. For it needs propositions (as opposed to names) to represent material properties; such properties are 'only formed by the configuration of the objects'. Red is a material property, and therefore formed by a configuration of objects—and, as I have said, by the *same configuration* of *different* objects in the different facts that exist when different things are red. These different objects, having the capacity to enter into configurations forming the material property red, will be of the same logical form: that of objects whose configurations yield colours. (Hence colour is a 'form of objects': 2·0251).

This, then, will be why he immediately goes on to say: 'Two objects of the same logical form—apart from their external properties—are only distinct from one another in that they are different' (2.0233). The only 'external properties' his simple objects can have, of course, are those of actually occurring in certain facts.

Here Wittgenstein adds a remark, which may seem at first sight to contradict the previous one: 'Either a thing has properties that no other has, in which case one can mark it out from the others through a description without more ado, and point to it; or on the other hand there are several things with all their properties in common, and then it is absolutely impossible to point to one of them. For if nothing marks a thing out, I cannot mark it out—if I did, it would be marked out.' It is possible that he is here thinking of what is involved in e.g. distinguishing between and identifying particles of matter. It would be wrong to infer from this passage that he thinks that there cannot *be* two things with all their properties in common: at 5.5302 he is explicit that it makes *sense* to say that two objects have all their properties in common.

Frege's notion of concepts led him to the awkwardness of saying: 'The concept *horse* is not a concept'; for, in statements about 'the concept *horse*', the concept *horse* is not the reference of these words since they are not words being used predicatively as words that stand for a concept must be. Frege came to think[1] that any such statement

[1] I am informed of this by Mr. M. A. E. Dummett, who has read some of Frege's unpublished writings at Münster.

was ill-formed; a concept must not occur except predicatively. That is, we can speak of 'the animal that both the Derby winner for 1888 and the Derby winner for 1889 are', but this expression, like 'a horse' itself, can occur only predicatively; we cannot say: 'the reference of this expression is the concept *horse*'.

Wittgenstein would say the sign for a function *shewed* itself to be the sign for a function; that something falls under a formal concept like 'function' is for him something that cannot be said; and Frege's difficulties about 'the concept *horse*' explain the point of this. If you say that your expression 'the animal that both the Derby winners are' has a concept as its reference, you at once lay yourself open to the question 'what concept?', with only one possible answer: 'the concept *horse*'—yet this 'is not a concept'. But the formal concept is rightly represented by the type of variable used in: 'There is a ϕ such that both the Derby winners are ϕ': the variable employed expresses what Frege wanted to express by the phrase 'the concept', and yet saw he could not properly express in this way.

8

OPERATIONS

We must now consider Wittgenstein's remarks on operations. They have a special interest in connection with his rejection of the Frege-Russell assertion sign, and Wittgenstein arrived at them in grappling with the problem of the assertion sign as introduced by Frege.

Although this sign, '|—', is still in use in symbolic logic, it has not now the same meaning as it had for Russell and Frege; it now means 'is a theorem', and so can occur (as it could not in Russell and Frege) hypothetically: 'if |—p', i.e. 'if p is a theorem . . .'. Russell's use of the sign explicitly follows Frege's; for Frege, the assertion sign symbolizes the difference between the thought of something's being the case and the judgment that it *is* the case—it can thus never occur in an *if* clause. Frege has two arguments for its necessity, one weak and the other strong.

The weak argument is from the necessity of a distinction between entertaining an hypothesis (formulating the content of a judgment, having a 'sense' before one's mind) and asserting a proposition. He says that an actor on the stage, for example, is not asserting. At that rate, it would be an inexcusable *faux pas* to make an actor write the assertion sign before a proposition on a blackboard in a play! This argument need not delay us.

The strong argument—in the light of which we can understand Wittgenstein on operations—is that we must distinguish between the occurrence of a proposition in a conditional: 'if p, then q', or a disjunction: 'either p, or q', and its occurrence when we simply say that p. The distinction is an obvious one, but quite difficult to express; it is natural to say that we are distinguishing between the occurrence of the proposition, unasserted, as a component of an assertion, and its occurrence when it is itself asserted: and here the distinction we are trying to make is certainly not a psychological one. But we cannot say that 'p', when it occurs by itself and when it occurs in a disjunction, 'p v q', has a different sense; for from 'p v q' and '~q' we can infer 'p', and the proposition that stands by itself as the conclusion must be the very same proposition as occurred as a disjunct.

Russell[1] uses this point in his explanation of the 'non-psychological' sense of '*being asserted*', which is what according to him must accrue to a proposition (besides what it has just *qua* proposition) when it is used as a premise to prove something, or is (rightly) inferred as a conclusion from a premise. 'When we say *therefore*, we state a relation which can only hold between asserted propositions, and which thus differs from implication.'

Being asserted (in this 'logical' sense) is, for both Russell and Frege, something that cannot possibly attach to a proposition unless it is true. But it is more than its being true; for in the disjunction 'p or q' it may be that one or the other proposition is true, but neither is being asserted. In Frege's terminology, we might say that if an unasserted proposition is true, it is (in fact) a designation of the true; but in the asserted proposition the true is actually being presented to us as such, it is not just that some designation of it occurs in our discourse.

Wittgenstein says curtly: 'Frege's assertion sign "|—" is logically quite meaningless: in Frege (and in Russell) it only indicates that these authors hold the propositions so marked to be true' (4.442). We must therefore enquire how he deals with the problem raised by Russell, about *therefore*; and also with the difference between 'p' and 'q' by themselves and in 'p v q' or 'p⊃q'.

The first point, about *therefore*, is dealt with at 6.1263–4: 'It is clear in advance that the logical proof of a significant proposition and proof in logic [i.e. proof of a proposition of logic from another proposition of logic] must be quite different things. The significant proposition says something, and its proof shews that things are as it says; in logic every proposition is the form of a proof. Every

[1] *Principles of Mathematics*, §38.

proposition of logic is a symbolic representation of a *modus ponens*. (And the *modus ponens* cannot be expressed by a proposition.)'

That is to say, Wittgenstein takes the tautology

$$(p.p \supset q) \supset q$$

to be just another symbolic representation of the form of argument called *modus ponens*, viz.:

$$\begin{array}{l} p \\ p \supset q \\ \therefore q \end{array}$$

Now 'representation' is the term Wittgenstein uses of a picture: what a picture represents is its sense. So here he is saying that the implication '(p, and p implies q) implies q', is *as it were* a picture or proposition with the *modus ponens* as its sense.

Russell says: 'When we say *therefore*, we state a relation that can only hold between asserted propositions.' He means, among other things, that *therefore* is something we are wrong to say, unless the premises are true and the conclusion too. This idea finds an echo in a statement by Frege in his essay on negation: 'One cannot infer anything from a false thought.' But that is not true. What is true—and, of course, what Frege was referring to—is that one cannot *prove* anything from false premises; one can criticize a proof by saying that the premises are false or doubtful. But it is wrong to say that 'therefore' is being misused in a correct argument from false premises. To be sure, 'therefore' is the utterance of someone who is asserting one or more propositions that precede it, and one that follows it, and he is in error if he asserts what is false; he is not however committing a *further* error in using 'therefore' just because his premises are false and his conclusion, accordingly, perhaps false. If these are his errors, they do not import a further mistake into his 'therefore'.

We must of course distinguish between the way a proposition occurs when used to assert what it means, and the way it occurs when e.g. it is merely a subordinate clause in a proposition that is asserted (a clause, moreover, that may be false, though the whole proposition is true); it is a mistake, though it is natural, to describe this difference as a difference between a 'logically asserted' and a 'logically unasserted' proposition. We have here a necessary distinction, wrongly made. 'Assertion' has *only* a psychological sense. We might indeed perhaps accept 'logically asserted' and 'logically unasserted' as technical descriptions of different ways in which propositions may occur; but it can be no part of the requirements for being 'logically asserted' that a 'logically asserted' proposition be true, as both Frege and Russell thought; and once that feature of 'logically asserted' propositions is removed, the terms become a mere pair of labels, and cease even to have an air of being explanatory. 'Logical assertion' is no longer an extra feature attaching to a proposition, or added to its sense; we have no idea what it is; we only know when to *call* propositions 'asserted' in this sense.

But this is not the end of the matter: the difference, if it has only been labelled, demands both to be made clearer and to be explained. First, although you cannot prove anything unless you know something, you can construct the *modus ponens* that *would* be a proof *if* you found out that its premises are true. '*If* these premises are true, this conclusion is true' is then a description of this *modus ponens*; which I suppose is what Wittgenstein meant by his remark (6.1264). The premises that you construct may be quite hypothetical; or again, you may know one premise and make an hypothesis of the other. This is the reason why Aristotle rightly says a conclusion is reached in just the same way in a 'demonstrative' and a 'dialectical' syllogism: if you say 'suppose p, and suppose q, then r'; or if, being given 'p', you say: 'suppose q, then r'; you are just as much inferring, and in essentially the same way, as if you are given 'p' and 'q' as true and say '*therefore* r'.

This, Wittgenstein would say, is because 'the structures of (the) propositions stand in internal relations to one another' (5.2). For at 5.131 he has said: 'If the truth of one proposition follows from the truth of others, this is expressed by relations in which the forms of those propositions stand to one another. . . . These relations are internal and exist simultaneously with, and through, the existence of the propositions.'

Wittgenstein goes on (at 5.21) to say that we can 'emphasize these internal relations in our form of expression, by representing one proposition as the result of an operation that produces it out of others (the bases of the operation)'. This is perhaps best explained in a simple, but not quite familiar, example. Take a relation and its converse, e.g. 'husband of' and 'wife of', and consider the two propositions: 'a is husband of b', 'a is wife of b'. We now introduce an operation, called 'conversion', the sign of which is 'Cnv' placed before a relative term; thus, instead of writing e.g. 'bRa', we write 'aCnvRb'. Then 'aCnv(husband of)b' emphasizes the internal relations of two propositions 'a is husband of b' and 'a is wife of b' by exhibiting the second proposition as the result of an operation upon the first (of course, an operation that could only be performed on propositions of this relational form).

An operation must not be assumed to be necessarily an inferential operation. In our present case, indeed, since 'husband of' is an asymmetrical relation, the two propositions are incompatible. An operation upon a given proposition as base may produce one that is compatible or incompatible with the proposition operated on; the only thing it does not produce is something equivalent to the proposition operated on. An operation is what has to happen to a proposition in order to turn it into a *different* one (cf. 5.23). And 'the operation is the expression of a relation between the structures of its result and of its base' (5.22).

In this example we can also understand clearly enough what is meant by saying: 'The occurrence of an operation does not characterize the sense of a proposition. For the operation does not assert anything, only its result does, and this depends on the bases of the operation' (5.25). It is very clear in this instance that 'Cnv' is not a distinguishing mark of the sense of a proposition, as 'not' might easily be thought to be; for you might think you can pick out a special class of *negative propositions*, but you would not be tempted to think that you can pick out a special class of *relations that are converses; every* relation has a converse, and is thus the converse of its converse, and can be written 'CnvR' for some suitable interpretation of 'R'.

Having grasped the general notion of an 'operation', we can now proceed to the next step, which is taken at 5.234: 'The truth-functions of the elementary propositions are the results of operations with the elementary propositions as bases. (I call these operations truth-operations).'

To say this is to make a radical distinction between a truth-function and an ordinary function like 'ϕx'. For as we have seen, Wittgenstein says that 'the occurrence of an operation is not a distinguishing mark of the sense of a proposition: for the operation does not assert anything, only its result does'. Now a function of names is certainly a distinguishing mark of the proposition in which it occurs: such a function certainly expresses something, marks out a form and a content. But the sign of an operation not merely stands for nothing—has no reference—it does not even mark out a form: it only marks the difference between forms.

Consider the following propositions which have 'p' and 'q' as bases of truth-functional operations:

$$p \vee q$$
$$p . q$$

Each of these can be written differently, e.g. we have the same pair of propositions in

$$\sim(\sim p . \sim q)$$
$$\sim(\sim p \vee \sim q)$$

For the first of the pair, we have here two versions: in one the proposition reached is shewn as the result of disjunction performed on 'p' and 'q'; in the other as the result of negation performed on the result of conjoining the results of negation performed on 'p' and 'q'; this is sufficient to shew that the mere occurrence of disjunction, or conjunction, or negation, is not a distinguishing mark of a proposition. On the other hand, if you perform a different operation on the very same base, you get a difference of sense.

Let us now compare Wittgenstein's position with those taken up by Frege and Russell. For Russell, a truth-function is one kind among the functions that take propositions as arguments. Frege places no such restrictions on what can be an argument; as we have seen, he constructs a function whose value is the true if a designation of the true occupies the argument-place, and is otherwise the false; and another function whose value is the false for those arguments for which the value of the previous function is the true, and *vice versa*. He finally constructs a third function:

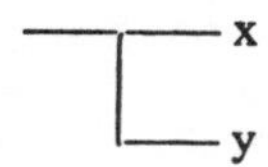

whose value is to be the false if we put a true proposition into the 'y' argument-place, and any designation which is *not* of the true (i.e. either a false proposition, or any designation other than a proposition) into the 'x' argument-place; in all other cases the value of the function is to be the true. This is material implication: 'either not p or q'.

Thus both for Frege and for Russell a truth-function is the same kind of thing as a function with an empty place for a name; but there is still a certain difference between Frege and Russell. For Frege, the empty place is a place for a *name*; propositions are counted among names, for he takes propositions (whose components all have reference) as names of truth-values. For Russell, propositions are just the range of significant substitutions for the variable in this kind of function; and he would not call a proposition a name. Further, he does not construct a function and stipulate what its values are to be for various arguments; he simply defines each of the truth-functions as 'that function which with argument p or arguments p and q (these being propositions) is the proposition that . . .', filling up the *that* clause with some statement about the truth or falsehood of the argument(s) like 'p is not true' or 'p and q are both true'.

Both Frege and Russell, however, would hold that the truth-functional connectives themselves express functions. For Wittgenstein it is otherwise. We saw earlier that to say: 'A proposition is a function of the expressions it contains' is not incompatible with saying: 'A proposition is not a function.' To say that a proposition is a function of the expressions it contains is to say that it is the result of completing them with one another. To say it is not a function is to say that it is not itself something with an empty place awaiting completion. In this sense of course a proposition that is a truth-function *of* others is not a function, on any view. But on Wittgenstein's view we must go further: a truth-function of propositions is not a function *of those propositions*; for it is the result of an *operation*, not a result of completing one expression with another; and a truth-argument is not the argument of a function, but the base on which an operation is performed. At 5.25–5.251 it is said explicitly: 'Operation and function must not be confused. A function cannot be its own argument, but the result of an operation can be the base of that very operation.' For example, we cannot put 'x is a man' into the argument-place in 'x is a man' itself—we get the nonsense 'x is a man is a man'; but we can write '∼p' for 'p' in '∼p' itself, and the result '∼ ∼p' makes perfect sense. Similarly, any operation may be iterated, any number of times. Sometimes an operation cancels out when it is iterated: '∼ ∼p' reduces to 'p', and 'aCnv(CnvR)b' to 'aRb' (*see* 5.254). A genuine function never behaves in this way.

With this we come to the question: What is the 'occurrence' of a proposition 'in' a complex proposition, which we have seen to be wrongly characterized as the occurrence of an unasserted in an asserted proposition? Wittgenstein's answer is that in the complex proposition its component proposition has the role *only of a truth-argument*: i.e. it is the base of a truth-operation.

We were inclined to argue: 'In "∼p" the *sense* of "p" must occur, but it is not being asserted, so we must distinguish between the sense of "p" and the assertion; here "assertion" has a non-psychological import, and signifies something that we add to the sense of "p" when we assert *that* p.' But Wittgenstein says: 'the sense of a truth-function of p is a function of the sense of p' (5.2341); here he is certainly making an arithmetical comparison: as 2 is a function of 4, namely its square root, so the sense of '∼p' is a certain function of the sense of 'p', and the sense of 'p' only occurs in that of '∼p' in the way in which 4 occurs in 2.

The difference, then, that we first wanted to call the difference between an asserted and an unasserted proposition—because we wished to say that the *sense* of 'p' must occur in '∼p' or in 'p v q'—is rightly described as a difference between the occurrence of the sense, and the occurrence, not of the sense, but of a certain function of the sense.

The argument by which we reached the view that 'assertion' was an extra feature which somehow gets added to the sense—' "p" must mean p, in "∼p" and "p v q", which nevertheless do not assert that p'—could be compared to arguing: ' "7" must mean 7 in "I had 7–3 apples"; so we must distinguish, even in empirical propositions where numerals occur, between the use of a numeral to designate a number of things, which we will call its positive use, and uses where it has the same sense but does not designate a number of things. Some extra feature therefore attaches to the use of the numeral in "I had 7 apples", but not in "I had 7–3 apples".' By this argument, we might propose to symbolize that 'extra feature' by prefixing the sign 'P' for 'positive' to certain occurrences of numerals, and think it necessary to write: 'I had P7 apples' and 'I had P (7–3) apples'.

9

FORMAL CONCEPTS AND FORMAL SERIES

At the end of his life, as we saw, Frege came to think that if something is a concept, we cannot correctly *say* that it is a concept—i.e. predicate the term 'concept' of it—because an expression for a concept can significantly occur only in the place of a predicate, not as a subject of the predicate 'concept'. This doctrine was what Wittgenstein expressed by saying: 'Something's falling under a formal concept, as an object[1] belonging to it, cannot be expressed by a proposition, but is rather shewn by the sign for that object' (4.126); e.g. if something falls under the 'formal' concept *concept* or *property*, this is shown by the predicative character of the sign we use for that 'something'; and again, a variable relating to properties will have to be one that we take as having one or more argument-places.

[1] This use of the term 'object' must not mislead us into thinking we have some evidence for Wittgenstein's counting properties and relations as objects, of different 'type' from the objects they attach to (contrary to the view stated in Chapter 7). It is the same use as Wittgenstein adopts, but apologizes for, at 4.123: 'A property is internal if its not belonging to its object is inconceivable. (This blue and that blue *eo ipso* stand in the internal relation of brighter and darker. It is inconceivable for *these* objects not to stand in this relation.) (To the shift in the use of the words "property" and "relation" there answers here a shift in the use of the word "object").' Just as internal properties and relations are not properly speaking properties and relations, so neither are shades of blue objects in the proper sense.

It may be asked: Why then did Wittgenstein resort to this misleading terminology? The answer, I think, is that the terminology of objects' falling under concepts is less loaded with philosophical doctrine, and more of a familiar way of speaking, in German than in English. Mr. Michael Dummett tells me that at Münster railway station he saw a notice beginning: 'All objects that fall under the concept *hand-luggage*' (*Alle Gegenstände, die unter den Begriff Handgepäck fallen*).

In Wittgenstein, as we saw (Chapter 5, pp. 82–3), the notion of a 'formal' concept, a concept that cannot be properly expressed by a predicate or general term, but only by the way we apply the corresponding sort of sign, is extended much more widely than this. Not only 'concept', 'function', 'object', but also 'number', 'fact', 'complex', are formal concepts; and, in opposition to Carnap, Wittgenstein would maintain that such linguistic concepts as 'name', 'predicate', 'proposition', 'relational expression' are also formal concepts. In none of these cases can it be informatively said of something that it falls under the concept; the only proper way of expressing a formal concept is (as Frege held for the concepts 'object', 'concept', 'function') the use of a special style of variable; and what makes a style of variable special is not (say) belonging to a special alphabet, but something that comes out in the use of the variable. If any proposition 'ϕA' contains a symbol 'A' for something falling under a formal concept, then we may always introduce the appropriate style of variable into the two blanks of '(E—)ϕ—' or 'For some—, ϕ—'. Thus: 'Socrates is snubnosed and bald'—'For some x, x is snubnosed and x is bald.' 'Socrates is bald and Plato is not'—'For some f, Socrates is f and Plato is not f.' 'Ten men mowed the meadow'—'For some *n*, *n* men mowed the meadow.' Thus: 'Along with an object falling under a formal concept, that concept is itself already given' (4.12721); the concept *object* is given by using 'Socrates', the concept *property* by using 'bald', the concept *number* by using 'ten'; and in each case the formal concept is to be symbolically expressed by a style of variable (4.1272).

As regards the formal concepts that he himself recognized, Frege so constructed his logical notation that inappropriate substitutions for the corresponding variables gave a visibly ill-formed expression; he had no need to appeal to what the signs were supposed to stand for, but only to formal rules. Russell abandoned this ideal for a symbolic language, and his system requires at critical points that he should tell us in English how the interpretation of his signs is to restrict their use; Wittgenstein sharply criticizes him for this at 3.33–.331 and again at 5.452. But Frege's own system does not, on Wittgenstein's view, satisfy the ideal; if 'ϕ( )' is a predicate, the empty place in it can according to Frege be filled up with *any* 'proper name', and for Frege 'proper names' include ordinary proper names, clauses in sentences, definite descriptions, and numerals. The fact that we should not ordinarily attach any sense at all to '(a rose is a rose) is white' or '7 is white' did not worry Frege; the concept *white*, he says, can be handled in logic only if we can stipulate, as regards any possible subject for the predicate 'white', what would be the condition for the predicate's holding; and *any* 'proper name' is such a possible subject. It was this sort of paradox that Russell sought to avoid by appealing to 'ranges of significance'; but Wittgenstein thought this remedy worse than the disease, because logic cannot rest on vague intuitions expressed in the vernacular about what is 'significant', but 'must take care of itself' (5.473).

Wittgenstein's own remedy was to give a wholly new account of the formal concepts 'proposition' and 'number', which should of itself show the mistake of treating clauses and numerals as proper names of objects. This account brings in the notion of a *formal series*. The doctrine underlying this notion is that operations, in the sense of the word explained in the last chapter, can be iterated—'the result of an operation can be the base of that very operation' (5.251). For example if we double a number, we can double the result. If we take 'O' to be an arbitrary operation, then starting from a base 'a' we get the formal series 'a, Oa, OOa, OOOa, . . .'[1]; and Wittgenstein represents an arbitrary term of this series by '[a, x, Ox]', where the first of the three expressions within the square brackets represents the first term of the series, and the other two represent the way of getting from each term on to the next. In important cases, the variable expressing a formal concept will relate to the terms of a formal series; Wittgenstein holds that this is so for the formal concept 'number' and (as we shall see in the next chapter) for the formal concept 'proposition' also.

[1] I omit the apostrophe that Wittgenstein puts after symbols of operation to indicate that he is speaking of *the result of the operation*: this is a vestige of the apostrophe used by Russell, who writes 'R'a' for 'the R of a'. In Russell this is significant, because '–Ra' is the predicate 'is an R of a', whereas 'R'a' is a definite description. In Wittgenstein it is superfluous and therefore meaningless, since operations are in any case sharply distinguished from relations. Nor is it used very consistently in the printed version of the *Tractatus*.

One might thus well think that for the concept 'number' it would have been enough for Wittgenstein to say as he does at 6.022–.03: 'The concept "number" is the variable number. . . . The general form of the whole number is $[0,\xi, \xi+1]$'—so long as this was supplemented by some account of '0' and of the special operation '+1'. In fact Wittgenstein goes about it in quite a different way. At 6.02 he gives the following definitions:

$$\Omega^0 x = x; \Omega^{n+1} x = \Omega\Omega^n x$$

This explains the meaning of a zero exponent of the operator 'Ω' and also the meaning of an exponent of the form 'n+1' given the meaning of the exponent 'n'.[1] He then defines the ordinary numerals in terms of 0 and +1, as follows:

$$1=0+1; 2=0+1+1; 3=0+1+1+1; \text{etc.}$$

This enables us to interpret the use of any ordinary numeral as an exponent; e.g. $\Omega^3 x = \Omega\Omega\Omega x$. And a number is always 'the exponent of an operation' (6.021); sentences where numerals appear to have other uses must be translatable into sentences where they occur as exponents—e.g. '2+2=4' into '$\Omega^2\Omega^2 x = \Omega^4 x$' (cf. 6.241). The formal concept 'term of such-and-such a formal series' just is the concept 'result of applying such-and-such an operation *an arbitrary number of times* to such-and-such a base', and a number is an exponent of *any* such operation; it would thus involve a vicious circle to treat numbers as just one special case of formal series. The informal way of writing the general term of a formal series, '$[x,\xi, \Omega\xi]$', (whose informal character is shown by the use of 'ξ', just as in Frege), is thus replaced by:

$$[\Omega^0 x, \Omega^n x, \Omega^{n+1} x] \text{ (6.02)}^1.$$

[1] He uses here a capital omega, instead of a Roman O as in other places, because 'O^0', where the big O is the sign of the operation and the exponent is 0, is disagreeably unperspicuous. The use of a Greek ν, by assimilation to the use of 'Ω', is pointless.

Wittgenstein's reason for introducing numbers only here, when he has already often used the conception of a formal series, is that you can explain what is meant by 'an arbitrary term of a formal series' quite clearly without explicit mention of numbers: 'First we have a; then Oa—the result of performing a certain operation on a; then OOa—the result of performing it on Oa; then OOOa; *and so on*; "an arbitrary term" means "some term or other reached in this way".'

To give a concrete example: We might explain 'ancestor in the male line' by saying: 'There's my father, and my father's father, and my father's father's father, and so on.' 'The concept of the successive application of an operation is equivalent to the concept *and so on*' (5.2523). We have the concept of an arbitrary term of a formal series when we understand 'and so on' in connection with the series; e.g. for the series of relations: father, father's father, father's father's father . . .,[1] we know what its general term is when we know what 'and so on' (or the row of dots I have just written) means in connection with the series. But if we ask, as regards some term of such a series, *which* term it is, *which* performance of the generating operation the term results from, the interrogative 'which?' is really an ordinal interrogative (Latin *quotus*?) requiring an ordinal numeral as an answer.

For Frege and Russell, (*natural*) *number* was not a formal concept, but a genuine concept that applied to some but not all objects (Frege) or to some but not all classes of classes (Russell); those objects, or classes, to which the concept *number* applied were picked out from others of their logical type as being 0 and the successors of 0. The relation *successor of* was in turn defined by means of the relation *immediate successor of*; plainly these two are related in the same way as *ancestor* (*in the male line*) *of* and *father of*—the one relation is, as Russell says, the ancestral of the other in each case. This brings us to the Frege-Russell account (independently devised by each of them in essentially the same form) of what it is for one relation to be the ancestral of another.[2] For simplicity's

[1] The series of ancestors is not a formal series, of course; but the series of relations thus involved is one.

[2] The relevant passages can be found in Frege's *Foundations of Arithmetic*, §§79–80, and in Russell and Whitehead's *Principia Mathematica*, Vol. I, Part II, Section E.

sake, I shall merely explain how *ancestor* would be defined in terms of *parent*; the generalization of this account can readily be supplied.

We first define the notion of a *hereditary* property: viz. a property which, if it belongs to one of a man's parents, belongs also to him. We then define 'a is an Ancestor of b' to mean:

'a is a parent of some human being, say x, all of whose hereditary properties belong to b.'

Let us for the moment treat this as an arbitrary verbal stipulation of what the defined term 'Ancestor' is to mean; we must now enquire whether it is true that, on this definition, a is an Ancestor of b if and only if a is in the ordinary sense an ancestor of b; if so, we have an adequate definition of ordinary ancestorship which does not introduce the 'and so on' brought into our ordinary explanations of the term (cf. the last paragraph but two). And it is quite easy to show intuitively that this equivalence between 'Ancestor' and 'ancestor' does hold.

A. Suppose a is an ancestor of b. Then either (1) a is a parent of b, or (2) a is a parent of an ancestor of b.

(1) If a is a parent of b, then b himself fulfils the conditions of being a human being, x, whose parent is a and whose hereditary properties all belong to b. So a is an Ancestor of b by our definition.

(2) If a is a parent of some human being x, who is b's ancestor, then the hereditary properties of x will all descend, through a finite number of generations, to b; so once again a will be a parent of some human being x whose hereditary properties all belong to b—i.e. will be an Ancestor of b.

Hence, if a is an ancestor of b, a is an Ancestor of b.

B. Suppose a is an Ancestor of b. Then there is some human being, x, whose parent is a and whose hereditary properties all belong to b. But *the property of having* a *as an ancestor is itself a hereditary property*, since any human being, one of whose parents has a as an ancestor, himself has a as an ancestor; hence, since this hereditary property belongs to x, and all hereditary properties of x belong to b, this property belongs to b—i.e. b has a as an ancestor.

Hence, if a is an Ancestor of b, a is an ancestor of b.

The italicized assertion in proof B may well make the reader suspect a vicious circle; if we are attempting a definition of ancestorship, how can we without circularity, in a proof that the definition is adequate, bring in properties that are themselves defined in terms of ancestorship? In an informal argument to show that a formal definition fits our ordinary idea of ancestorship, this might, to be sure, not seem to matter very much; for we are anyhow supposed to know informally what 'ancestor' means, and it is 'ancestor', not 'Ancestor' the formally defined term, that is the word used in specifying the questionable 'hereditary property'. This threat of circularity is, however, not found only in informal arguments; in *Principia Mathematica* some of the theorems and proofs formally and explicitly assume that the properties that are hereditary with respect to a relation R include some that are themselves defined in terms of that ancestral relation which corresponds to R as *Ancestor* corresponds to *parent*.[1] Wittgenstein's accusation of having run into a vicious circle about the ancestral relation (4.1273) was a peculiarly vicious blow against Russell, who had elaborately contrived the system of *Principia* in order to avoid circles of this sort (*see op. cit.*, Vol. I, Introduction, Ch. II). Russell came to be seriously worried by the accusation, and in the second edition of *Principia* he added as an appendix a new chapter of proofs designed to avoid the vicious circle.

Wittgenstein himself did not need the analysis of ancestral relations in order to give an account of the number-concept; but such relations are logically important in their own right, and supplied him with an application for his notion of a formal series. It is clear that the series of propositions

aRb; (Ex) aRx.xRb; (Ey) (Ex) aRx.xRy.yRb;
and so on

is a formal series in Wittgenstein's sense, as he says (4.1273). He does

[1] *op. cit.*, Vol. I, *90.163, *90.164, and proof of *90.31. (To make this strictly correct, one would have to modify slightly the definition of 'Ancestor' so as to count also as his own Ancestor anyone who either was or had a parent.)

not, however, tell us what operation must be applied to each term to yield the next one; and if we use 'x', 'y', etc. as variables, the operation is not perspicuously displayed. For here 'what the signs conceal, their use reveals'; it is the case, though the style of variables here used conceals it, that we have to think of variables as *themselves* forming an indefinitely long series, a *formal* series, in which each variable is derived from its predecessor; otherwise our capacities of expression would run out as soon as we had used all the letters of the alphabet. 'The same operation turns the variable "p" into the variable "q", "q" into "r", and so on. This can only be explained by these variables' giving general expression to certain formal relations' (5.242). Wittgenstein's idea of an unlimited stock of variables, given once for all by a formal rule, is taken for granted in modern discussions of logical syntax.

The series may be exhibited more clearly as a formal series by using 'x, x′, x″, x‴, . . .' instead of 'x, y, z, . . .' as variables, and writing the terms of the series as follows:

$$(Ex')\ (Ex)\ a=x.xRx'.x'=b$$
$$(Ex'')\ (Ex')\ (Ex)\ a=x.xRx'.x'Rx''.x''=b$$
$$(Ex''')\ (Ex'')\ (Ex')\ (Ex)\ a=x.xRx'.x'Rx''.x''Rx'''.x'''=b$$

and so on.[1]

Indeed, it would be quite easy to put into words a formal rule for deriving each successive line from the last line. If we use ר (Hebrew Resh) as a symbol of the operation successively applied, the general term of this formal series will be written in Wittgenstein's style as:

$$[ר^{0}p,\ ר^{n}p,\ ר^{n+1}p]$$

where 'p' is '(Ex′) (Ex) a=x.xRx′.x′=b'. And to say that b

[1] Remember that 'a=x' means that a is the same thing as x; and 'x′=b', that x′ is the same thing as b.

is a successor of a with respect to the relation R will be to assert the logical sum of this formal series of propositions—i.e. to assert that some proposition or other in the series is true.[1]

Wittgenstein used his doctrine of formal series to make a further important criticism of Russell and Whitehead: that they kept on making tacit use of formal series whose component propositions were, on their own theory, propositions of different 'logical type' and as such could not form a single series (5.252). One example of this fallacy occurs in their use of the Axiom of Reducibility. This axiom may be stated as follows: *For any property of individuals that is specified in terms of quantification over properties of individuals,*[2] *there is another property that applies to the same individuals and is not specified in terms of such quantification.*[3]

Now at *20.112 Russell requires, not this axiom, but a parallel axiom got by substituting '*properties of individuals*' throughout for '*individuals*'; yet he simply refers back to the Axiom of Reducibility for individuals (in fact he merely gives its number, *12.1). Clearly he would in strictness need a new Axiom for properties of individuals, and another for properties of properties of individuals, *and so on*—i.e. a formal series of axioms, each constructed in a uniform way from its predecessor; and the only legitimate way of supplying what is required would be to give the generating operation of this series. But Russell's Theory of Types explicitly rules out the possibility of

[1] In his paper 'On Derivability', *Journal of Symbolic Logic*, Vol. II, No. 3 (September 1937), Quine shews that a certain notion, practically the same as that of a formal series of expressions, enables us to define ancestral relations without any such quantifications as 'every property that . . .' or 'some one of the relations . . .' at all. This definition, which may be called a fulfilment of Wittgenstein's intentions, accordingly avoids any risk of a vicious circle, such as might arise if some of the properties or relations covered by the quantifications employed had themselves to be specified in terms of the ancestral relation.

[2] e.g. the property of having *all* the properties of a great general; or again, the property of having *all* the vices of Charles I and *none* of his virtues.

[3] The property of *being* a great general applies to the same individuals as the property of *having all the properties of* a great general; but is not itself specified, as that property is, in terms of quantification over properties of individuals.

such an operation, since each successive proposition in the series would be of higher 'type' than its predecessor, and not groupable with it in a single series.[1] Unlike the criticism about ancestral relations, this criticism was ignored by Russell in preparing the second edition of *Principia Mathematica.*

[1] Wittgenstein's objection that the Axiom of Reducibility would not be a *logical* truth anyhow (6.1233) is independent, and not here relevant. For a clear modern account of *this* problem, see Quine's *From a Logical Point of View*, Chapter VI, §6.

10

'THE GENERAL FORM OF PROPOSITION'

It is now possible to explain the formula $[\bar{p}, \bar{\xi}, N(\bar{\xi})]$ which Wittgenstein gives as 'the general form of truth-functions'. Russell's explanation given in the Introduction is useless and should be disregarded. Anyone with a taste for exegesis for its own sake will be able to work out how Russell came to give this explanation, which was probably prompted by an answer given by Wittgenstein to a question of his: 'What is ξ here?'

The formula is a particular example of the 'general term of a formal series', with a set of propositions as the first term and joint negation as the generating operation. We have seen that the presence of ξ in a formula is the mark of informal exposition; hence, once we can use numbers, this formula can be given as

$$[\bar{p}, N^{n}(\bar{p}), N^{n+1}(\bar{p})]$$

$\bar{p}$[1] is the whole collection of elementary propositions; the formula therefore presupposes that if the number of elementary propositions were finite, we could say exactly what, say, the hundred and third term of the series of truth-functions (whose general term this formula is) would be.

Let us consider the case of only two elementary propositions, p and q, and shew how the totality of the truth-functions of p and q can be generated by 'successive applications' of the operation $N(\bar{\xi})$. The

[1] The stroke over the variable indicates that the variable stands for an arbitrarily stipulated list of propositions which are the values of the variable (*see* 5.501). These are a mere list, and hence not a single proposition except in the degenerate case where the list has only one item. The application of the operation $N(\bar{\xi})$ to the values of the variable, on the other hand, always results in a single proposition.

general term of the formal series of truth-functions having p andqa s truth-arguments will be

$$[p,q, N^{n}(p,q), N^{n+1}(p,q)]$$

We can easily state the second, third, fourth, etc. up to the seventeenth term of this series; it has only seventeen terms; for there are fourteen distinct truth-functions of p and q, plus tautology and contradiction. The first term, 'p,q', is of course not a truth-function and not a proposition; it is just a list of the bases of the operation. The second term, and first truth-function, in the series is N(p,q) (=neither p nor q); and the second truth-function is the result of applying the operation to the result of the first application of it: it is therefore N(N(p,q)), i.e. p v q.

If we applied the operation once more to this result, we should only get back to the first truth-function, since ∼ ∼p=p. So we apply the operation to the two results obtained so far, and obtain N(N(p,q), N(N(p,q))), which, being the joint denial of a pair of contradictories, is contradiction. The next result will be obtained by applying the operation to this last-obtained result, i.e. negating it, and is tautology.

If we now apply the operation to the last two results as values of ξ, the result is once again contradiction, which we have already got, so we discard it. And if we apply the operation to the third result, contradiction, together with the first, we get tautology conjoined with the negation of the first result, which is the same as the second result; similarly if we apply the operation to the third result, contradiction, together with the second, we get tautology conjoined with the negation of the second, which is the same as the first result. Similarly it is fruitless to apply the operation to the fourth result, tautology, in any combination, since this will always yield contradiction. And if we now proceed to make the first four results, first in such threes as are possible, and then all at once, the subject of the operation, we shall reach no new result.

For our next truth-function we therefore bring down the first of the bases, combining it with the result of the first application, and write N((N(p,q)),p), i.e. ∼(∼p.∼q).∼p, i.e. p v q.∼p, i.e. q. The next application, N(N((N(p,q)),p), negates the previous one and yields

$\sim$q; no more can be done by a reapplication of the operation to the result so obtained, which will only give us q again. We therefore try bringing our base, p, into combination with the result of the second application of $N(\bar{\xi})$. This was N(N(p,q)), and we write

$$N((N(N(p,q))),p)$$

which gives us $\sim$(p v q).$\sim$p, i.e. $\sim$p.$\sim$q.$\sim$p. But that is the same as $\sim$p.$\sim$q, which we have already had; so it adds nothing, and neither will its negation.

At the next step we take as values of ξ the result of the third application, which was contradiction, and our first base, p; now N(contradiction, p) is (tautology.$\sim$p), which is the same as $\sim$p. The result of the next application will of course be the negation of this, i.e. p.

We next take as values of ξ the result of the fourth application, tautology, and p; but this gives us (contradiction.$\sim$p), which is still contradiction, and the negation of it will be tautology.

When we have gone as far as we can with our first base and previous results, we bring down our second base, q, and combine it with the result of the first application; this will yield p, and an application of $N(\bar{\xi})$ to this its negation, $\sim$p; having reached these already, we discard them.

We go on in this way until no new application of the operation to results hitherto reached, together with our second base, yields any proposition not already obtained. We go on taking as values of ξ any results not hitherto taken together—of course we are not confined to only one or two values for ξ at a time, but use all possible numbers in a systematic order. It is clear that we can have here a series with a definite order, if we suppose that we are given the original bases in a definite order. This of course is the precise reason why Wittgenstein says at 5.242 that ' "p", "q" and "r" must be variables which give general expression to certain formal relations'. The use in symbolism of the variable propositional signs p, q, r must bring these formal relations out; and they would be brought out most clearly if we wrote p′, p″, p‴, etc.

That Wittgenstein's account makes sense for any finite set of bases is clear enough. What was needed was that the description 'the result of the nth application of the operation $N(\xi)$ to these bases' should be an absolutely precise determination of a proposition for any number n up to the total number of truth-functions that there are for this set of bases. It is clear that it is such a precise determination of a proposition.

Here we come to the defect in the *Tractatus* which Wittgenstein described, later, as a failure to distinguish between the 'dots of laziness', as when we represent the alphabet by writing just 'A,B,C, . . .', and the indispensable dots used to represent an infinite series, as in '1,2,3,4, . . .'. It is easy to see how he came not to make this distinction, if we consider the following diagram:

p	q	r	s	t	v	.	.	.	.	.	.	.	
T	T	T	T	T	T	T	T	T	T	T	T	.	F
F	T	T	T	T	T	T	T	T	T	T	T	.	F
T	F	T	T	T	T	T	T	T	T	T	T	.	F
F	F	T	T	T	T	T	T	T	.	.	.	.	F
T	T	F	T	T	T	.	.	.	.	.	.	.	F
F	T	F	T	T	T	.	.	.	.	.	.	.	F
T	F	F	T	T	T	.	.	.	.	.	.	.	F
F	F	F	T	T	T	.	.	.	.	.	.	.	F
T	T	T	F	T	T	.	.	.	.	.	.	.	F
F	T	T	F	T	T	.	.	.	.	.	.	.	F
.	.	.	(8 F's)	(16 T's)	(32 T's)								.
.	.	.	.	.	.								.
.	.	.	.	.	.								.
.	.	.	.	.	.								.
.	.	.	.	.	.								.
.	.	.	.	.	.								.
.	.	.	.	.	.								.
.	.	.	(8 F's)	(16 F's)	(32 F's)								.
T	T	F	F	F	F	F	F	.	.	.	.	.	F
F	T	F	F	F	F	F	F	.	.	.	.	.	F
T	F	F	F	F	F	F	F	.	.	.	.	.	F
F	F	F	F	F	F	F	F	.	.	.	.	.	T

(In the left-hand column, the T's and F's alternate; in the second column they alternate in pairs, in the third in fours; and so on.)

This table represents a quite definite truth-function of a set of propositions of unspecified number; this truth-function has the truth-value *false* for all combinations of truth-values except the final one; it does not matter how many propositions there are, because the bottom line of arguments is all F's anyway. This truth-table defines, for an arbitrary number of bases, our operation $N(\bar{\xi})$—joint negation of all the propositions in the set; and the liberal use of dots in it may well seem not to matter—the rule for constructing the table is plain. If, therefore, the repeated application of this operation to the given bases will in any finite case generate all their truth-functions, and if it is possible to specify a set of propositions otherwise than by enumeration, then it is very natural to say: what does it matter that the number in the set is not known, what does it matter even if it is infinite?

There would indeed be a serious objection if operating thus upon the set of propositions did not generate a simple infinite series (a progression) but one that was e.g. like the set of odd numbers in natural order followed by the set of even numbers in natural order. That series can of course be rearranged as the progression 1,2,3,4, . . .; but it might be that without ceasing to be a formal series our series could not so be rearranged. In that case the expression 'the nth term of the series' would never, for any finite n, get you into the part of the series that began after you had started on a second infinite series. Hence, if in the generation of a series of truth-functions by repeatedly performing the operation $N(\bar{\xi})$ upon the set of elementary propositions (in the way I have described) there would have to be a series of generations which you could only begin *after* you had gone through the process of bringing down each new member of the set in turn, right to the end of the infinite set; then Wittgenstein's idea would be worthless.

But this difficulty can in fact never arise. You can perform the new operations on the terms up to the nth term, which are made possible by the introduction of the $n+1^{st}$ term, as soon as you have introduced the $n+1^{st}$ term; and there is never an infinity that you have to finish before you can get on, because you quickly generate propositions that either are tautologies or contradictions, or are identical with propositions you have already generated, and you do not have to proceed further with those. You clear up as you go along.

On the other hand, the claim that is being made, in offering this as the general term of the series of truth-functions of an infinite set of elementary propositions, is apparently in conflict with the well-known theorem that the truth-functions of an infinite set of elementary propositions form a non-denumerable set. This is so, because the number of different assignments of truth-values to n propositions is 2^n. The number of different assignments of truth-values to $\aleph_0$ propositions (i.e. to a denumerably infinite set of propositions) is therefore $2^{\aleph_0}$. But this has been proved by Cantor to be greater than $\aleph_0$; that is to say, you could not find a one-one correlation between a set whose number was $2^{\aleph_0}$ and a set whose number was $\aleph_0$. And the truth-functions of $\aleph_0$ propositions must be *at least* as many as the possible ways of assigning truth-values to them. Therefore an account which correlates the series of truth-functions of an infinite set of elementary propositions with the series of natural numbers, as Wittgenstein's does, must be wrong.

It seems likely enough, indeed, that Wittgenstein objected to Cantor's result even at this date, and would not have accepted a Cantorian device for specifying an infinite subset of the elementary propositions such that a truth-function of it could not be generated by his formula. For though he came to think his idea wrong, it was certainly not through any conversion to Cantor that this happened. On the contrary: whether or no he already objected to Cantor at the time when he wrote the *Tractatus*, he certainly did so later.

However, the theory of the *Tractatus*, promising though it looked at the time, has been clearly and cogently refuted in another way. If all truths of logic are tautological truth-functions of elementary propositions, then there is in principle a decision procedure for them all. But it was proved by Church in the 1930's that multiple quantification theory has no decision procedure; that is, that there cannot be a method by which one could settle, concerning any well-formed formula of that theory, whether it was a theorem or not.

11

GENERALITY

Frege's invention of the quantifier-notation must be reckoned among the greatest benefits conferred on philosophy by logic. The fallacies which are excluded by the insight it gives have been committed over and over again by the greatest philosophers. No one should now be able to get away with transitions like that from 'Every boy loves some girl' to 'Some girl is loved by every boy'. In this down-to-earth example, the fallacy sounds silly and impossible to commit; in abstract contexts, it and similar fallacies (involving the notions, not just of 'some' and 'all', but of one of these combined with 'necessary', or 'possible') have proved very difficult to avoid.

A recent example of this sort of fallacy is afforded by Professor Ayer;[1] he argues from the fact that it is not possible, and *a fortiori* not necessary, that every identification or recognition (of a person, shape, quality, etc.) should in fact be checked, to the innocuousness of the notion of an uncheckable identification. An argument running 'It is not necessary that every identification is checkable; *ergo*, it is possible that some identification is uncheckable' has all the appearance of formal validity—'Not necessarily (every S is P); *ergo*, possibly (some S is not P)'. But in fact it is an illicit transition from:

(1) It is possible that it is not possible that every identification should be checked

to

[1] *The problem of knowledge*, pp. 60–1. The passage concerns Wittgenstein's objection (in *Philosophical Investigations*) to 'private' ostensive definition. Professor Ayer seems to accept a kind of checkability as necessary to the notion of an identification; but in reply to the objection that 'private' checks are not checks, he retorts that in any case checks always have to come to an end somewhere.

(2) It is possible that there should be some identification that it is not possible to check.

It is one of the uses of the quantifier-notation to make this clear. Let 'M' represent 'possibly'; (1) and (2) then come out as:

(1) $M \sim M(x)$ (x is an identification $\supset$ x is checked)

(2) $M(Ex)$ (x is an identification. $\sim M$ (x is checked))

or (equivalently): $M \sim (x)$ (x is an identification $\supset M$ (x is checked))

The quantifier-signs now in use, '$(x)\phi x$' for 'Everything is ϕ' and '$(Ex)\phi x$'[1] for 'Something is ϕ', were given us by Russell and Whitehead; but the former is a variation of Frege's generality notation, and the latter can be defined in terms of it, so the real inventor was Frege.

Often enough a logical symbolism simply puts some new sign in place of a word or phrase; this may be helpful. But what the quantifier-notation does is quite different. At first sight 'Everyone is clever' looks to be just such a sentence as 'Socrates is clever'. It becomes clear that it is not, as soon as we consider negation: if 'Socrates is clever' is untrue, then 'Socrates is not clever' is true; but, as Aristotle remarked, the same does not hold for 'Everyone is clever'. Frege's genius consisted in inventing a notation in which a formula of a different layout is employed for universal propositions; and not just of a different layout, but of the right layout.

This was surely partly what prompted Wittgenstein to say at 3.323: 'In ordinary language it is enormously common for . . . two words, which signify in different ways, to be applied in the sentence in ways that are outwardly the same. . . . In this way there easily arise the most fundamental confusions (with which the whole of philosophy is filled).

'In order to avoid these errors, we must use a symbolism which excludes them—A symbolism, then, that follows *logical* grammar—logical syntax'. And again, it will have been this that inspired the 'feeling' that he speaks of at 4.1213, the 'feeling that we are in possession of the right logical conception if only all is right in our symbolism'.

At 4.0411 Wittgenstein dilates on the excellence of the symbolism

[1] Russell and Whitehead actually use an inverted 'E'; I am following Hilbert and Ackermann.

'(x)fx'. He brings this out by considering alternative ways of expressing what we use this symbolism to express. We might try putting 'Gen.fx'; but 'this would not tell us what was generalized'. That is, it would be ambiguous as between what we should now write as '(x)fx' and '(f)fx'. If we try to make good this defect by writing the sign for generality as a subscript to the x, thus: '$f(x_g)$', it still would not do: 'we should not know the scope of the generality-sign': That is, '$\phi x_g \vee \psi x_g$' would be ambiguous as between '$(x)\phi x \vee (x)\psi x$' and '$(x)\phi x \vee \psi x$'. Finally, if we thought of writing the generality sign itself in the argument-place: (G,G)f(G,G) 'we should not be able to determine the identity of the variables'. That is to say, the expression

$$(G,G)\phi(G,G) \vee \psi(G,G)$$

would be ambiguous as between what we should now write as

$$(x,y)\phi(x,y) \vee \psi(x,y)$$

and

$$(x,y)\phi(x,y) \vee \psi(y,x).$$

In particular, we could not distinguish between these cases:

$$(x,y)\phi(x,y) \vee \sim\phi(x,y)$$

which holds for any relation ϕ, and

$$(x,y)\phi(x,y) \vee \sim\phi(y,x)$$

which means that the relation ϕ is symmetrical.

These difficulties could of course be got over by supplementary conventions, corresponding to the 'enormously complicated tacit conventions' which Wittgenstein mentions at 4.002 as needed for the understanding of ordinary language. Think of the English sentence 'If you can eat any fish, you can eat any fish', which sounds like a tautology, but is, on the contrary, a false judgment. Any native English-speaker will understand that sentence: few could explain how it works. And again e.g. 'You can fool some of the people all of the time' is ambiguous; the ambiguity is resolved, in some complicated way, by the context. It is clear that the Fregean quantifier-notation is far more perspicuous than any that has to be backed up with complicated conventions.

Turning now to Wittgenstein's special treatment of generality, we shall find it helpful to place the opening entry, 5.52, in juxtaposition with 5.51, the immediately preceding entry of the same numerical level in the book:

5.51: 'If ξ has only one value, then $N(\bar{\xi}) = \sim p$ (not p); if it has two values, then $N(\bar{\xi}) = \sim p . \sim q$ (neither p nor q).'

5.52: 'If the values of ξ are all the values of a given function fx for all values of x, then $N(\bar{\xi})$ will be the same as $\sim$(Ex)fx.'

Russell's account in the Introduction, then, is quite correct: 'Wittgenstein's method of dealing with general propositions [i.e. "(x)fx" and "(Ex)fx"] differs from previous methods by the fact that the generality comes only in specifying the set of propositions concerned, and when this has been done the building up of truth-functions proceeds exactly as it would in the case of a finite number of enumerated arguments p, q, r, . . .' Wittgenstein emphasizes the difference by saying: '*I* separate the concept *all* from the truth-function' and goes on to accuse Frege and Russell of not having done this: 'Frege and Russell introduced generality in connection with the logical product [p.q.r.——] or the logical sum [p v q v r v——]. This made it difficult to understand the propositions "(Ex)fx" and "(x)fx", which cover both ideas.'

Now there is no ground in their texts for a direct accusation that either Frege or Russell 'introduced generality in connection with the logical product or the logical sum'. We must therefore see in this remark Wittgenstein's comment on their way of introducing generality: a claim that this is what it amounts to. So we must examine how they actually introduce generality.

Frege introduced his generality notation in this way in *Function and Concept*: he constructs the sign

$$\underset{\smile}{\mathfrak{a}}\, f(\mathfrak{a})$$

in which what he has done is (to quote from his *Begriffsschrift*) to *replace an argument*, say 'London' in 'London is a capital city', '*with a German letter, and insert a concavity in the content stroke, and make this same German letter stand over the concavity*'.

The sign so constructed signifies the thought that '*The function is a fact whatever we take its argument to be.*' Or, as he puts it in *Function and Concept*, the sign

$$\underset{\smile}{\mathfrak{a}}\, f(\mathfrak{a})$$

is 'to mean the true when the function $f(x)$ always has the true as its value, whatever the argument may be'. Certainly there is nothing here about a logical product. So what is Wittgenstein's argument?

It is based on his own view: the truth of such a proposition as '(x)fx' (to use the signs now usual) is the truth of the logical product: 'fa.fb.fc.fd——' where the dots cover up our failure to write down all the names there are as arguments in the function fx. Therefore when Frege explains his symbol, by stating *what* is judged to be the case in the judgment that it symbolizes, he is in fact introducing 'all' in connection with the logical product.

Frege does not employ an existential quantifier like '(Ex)' in constructing the symbol for judgments of the form 'Some——'; he simply uses negation together with his universal quantifier, just as we can define '(Ex)fx' as '~(x)~fx'; but the same point would hold for the explanation of particular judgments: their truth—according to Wittgenstein—consists in the truth of a logical sum (fa v fb v fc v fd——) and hence what they say is that that logical sum is true. So someone who explains them by explaining what they say is 'introducing generality in connection with the logical sum'.

Russell's explanations are not relevantly different from Frege's.

'This,' Wittgenstein says, 'made it difficult to understand "(x)fx" and "(Ex)fx", which cover both ideas.' By 'both ideas' he means both the idea of generality on the one hand, and that of the logical product (in the case of universal propositions), or the logical sum (in the case of particular propositions), on the other. The reason why 'it became difficult to understand' these propositions was that their pictorial character was obscured. Their pictorial character consists in their being truth-functions of a set of propositions. But the notation also covers the way of *specifying* the set a truth-function of which is being asserted, viz. giving a function *all* of whose values are the set in question. 'The function's being a fact whatever we take the argument to be' explains generality in terms of the truth of the generalized proposition. With such an explanation, how are we to understand the inference from $(x)\phi x$ to ϕa; i.e. from something's holding of a function, to something's holding of an object? As Ramsey says, Wittgenstein's view 'explains how "fa" can be inferred from "For all x, fx", and "There is an x such that fx" from "fa". The alternative theory that "There is an x such that fx" should be regarded as an atomic proposition of the form "F(f)" ("f has application") leaves this entirely obscure; it gives no intelligible connection between *a* being red and red having application, but abandoning any hope of explaining this relation is content merely to label it "necessary".'[1]

Wittgenstein goes on to make further comments on the generality notation. It has, he says, two peculiarities: it points to a logical proto-picture, and it emphasizes constants. Ramsey explains the second point to us. 'Let us consider when and why an expression occurs, as it were, as an isolated unit. "aRb" does not naturally divide into "a" and "Rb", and we want to know why anyone should so divide it and isolate the expression "Rb". The answer is that if it were a matter of this proposition alone, there would be no point in dividing it in this way, but that the importance of expressions arises, as Wittgenstein points out, just in connection with generalization. It is not "aRb" but "(x)xRb" which makes "Rb" prominent. In writing (x)xRb we use the expression "Rb" to collect together the set of propositions xRb which we want to assert to be true; and it is here that the expression "Rb" is really essential because it is this which is common to this set of propositions.'[2]

Wittgenstein does not explicitly say that the importance of 'expressions' arises in connection with generalization: rather he uses the notion of an expression to form his theory of generality. For him expressions explain generality: an expression, by being 'the common

[1] *The Foundations of Mathematics*, pp. 153–4.
[2] Ramsey, *ibid.*, pp. 123–4.

characteristic mark of a class of propositions', gives us that class—the class of them all. But the class in question is clearly that narrower range of propositions in which an expression occurs, which Ramsey found it necessary to distinguish.

At 4.12721 Wittgenstein tells us: 'The formal concept is already given with an object that falls under it.' That is, if we have been given fa, the formal concept presented by the name-variable x is already given: the 'proto-picture' 'fx' is given. Here I assume that 'f' is a constant; thus this proto-picture is not the 'logical proto-picture' that is obtained by turning all the constants, into which a proposition divides up, into variables, as was described at 3.315: 'If we change one component of a proposition into a variable, then there is a class of propositions which are all values of the resulting variable proposition. This class in general still depends on what we, by arbitrary convention, mean by parts of that proposition. But if we change all those signs whose reference has been arbitrarily determined into variables, there is still always such a class. This, however, now no longer depends on convention; it depends only on the nature of the proposition. It corresponds to a logical form—a logical proto-picture': '(x)x moves slower than light', for example, *lays emphasis on* 'moves slower than light' as an expression which collects together a class of propositions, and *points to* a 'logical proto-picture' xRy, where (taking R as variable) all the constants have been turned into variables.

This paves the way for Wittgenstein's next remarks: 'The sign of generality appears as an argument. Once objects are given, that of itself gives us *all* objects. Once elementary propositions are given, that is enough for *all* elementary propositions to be given' (5.523–4). When he says 'the sign of generality occurs as an argument' he is referring to the 'x' in '$(x)\phi x$': we have passed from the form 'ϕa' to the construction of the form 'ϕ everything' which we can do because the expression '$\phi(\ )$' collects all propositions of the same form as 'ϕa': it determines a certain range of propositions. '$(x)\phi x$' is then just the proposition which is a certain truth-function of those propositions: we saw just why this should be so good a notation at the opening of the present chapter. Thus it is that we are formally given 'all objects'—and therewith the possibility of all their connections, which form the elementary situations—; and thus it is that we are given 'all elementary propositions', and therewith all possible propositions, i.e. all possibilities of being the case or not the case.

Wittgenstein's view has the following strong advantage. If we introduce 'v' as a truth-functional connective, then unless we adopt Wittgenstein's view we need a new account of it in such propositions as '$(x)\phi x \vee \psi x$'—e.g. 'All roses are either red or yellow', for here it does not conjoin clauses to which a truth-value can be assigned. 'If logic has primitive notions,' he says at 5.451, 'they must be inde-dependent of one another. If a primitive notion is introduced, it must be introduced for all the contexts in which it occurs at all. Thus we cannot introduce it first for *one* context, and then introduce it all over again for another. For example: If negation has been introduced, we must understand it in propositions of the form "$\sim p$" just as in propositions like "$\sim(p \vee q)$", "$(Ex)\sim fx$", etc. We cannot introduce it first for the one class of cases, and then for the other, for then it would be doubtful whether it meant the same in both cases, and there would be no ground for using the same kind of connective in both cases. In a word, what Frege said (in the *Grundgesetze der Arithmetik*) about the introduction of signs by means of definitions holds, *mutatis mutandis*, for primitive signs.' Russell and Whitehead did introduce '$\sim$' and 'v' all over again for uses with quantifiers (*see* Sections *9 and *10 of *Principia Mathematica*). Modern logicians mostly introduce them with a merely truth-functional explanation, and then go on using them 'with innocent faces'[1] in the predicate calculus.

The concept 'all' is all-pervasive in the *Tractatus*. 'The world is *everything* that is the case—the *totality* of facts—determined by the facts and by their being *all* the facts' (1–1.11). And at 4.51–2 we find: 'Suppose *all* elementary propositions were given me: then we can simply ask what propositions I can form from them. And these are *all* propositions: *that* is how they are limited. Propositions are: All that follows from the totality of elementary propositions (and of course from its being the *totality of them all*). Thus it might be said

[1] cf. *Tractatus*, 5.452. For an example, *see* Quine, *Methods of Logic*, Section 16.

that in a certain sense *all* propositions are generalizations of the elementary propositions.'

We have to think of the case in which the world is finite, remembering that Wittgenstein did not think there was any essential difference between the finite and the infinite case. If we want to say not merely that such-and-such things are green, but that everything (in a box, for example) is green, this can be expressed by saying: 'There are an x and a y in the box, x and y are green, and there are not an x and a y and a z in the box.' (Here I am using Wittgenstein's proposed convention about identity: 'Identity of the object I express by identity of the sign, not by a sign of identity: difference of the object by difference of the sign'[1] (5.53).) It is clear that 'Everything in the box is green' does not follow just from 'The objects a and b, which are in the box, are green': it must also be the case that a and b *are all the objects in the box*.

Similarly, that such-and-such an independent possibility is not the case follows from all the facts, together with the fact that these are all the facts. (As Professor Stenius has pointed out to me, at this stage (1.11) Wittgenstein means by 'the facts' only 'positive facts': he has not yet introduced the expression 'a negative fact' for the 'non-existence of atomic facts', but has only brought in 'facts' which are stated to consist in the existence of atomic facts.) And so Wittgenstein says: 'the totality of facts determines both what is the case and also all that is not the case' (1.12); and this is so whether the world is finite or infinite.

How this is so is seen clearly in the finite case; yet in the finite case Wittgenstein's doctrine appears to have a rather inconvenient consequence which Ramsey drew. Ramsey argues that 'There are an x and a y such that $x \neq y$' is the logical sum of the propositions $x \neq y$, which are tautologies if x and y have different values, contradictions if they have the same value. Hence it is itself a tautology

[1] He has sometimes been taken to *demand* this convention. This is a misunderstanding; he merely puts it forward as a possible one. The fact that (however inconvenient) it is possible shews that identity is not a genuine function. His view, then, does not require the abandonment of the sign of identity if it should be convenient to use it. But it does exclude uses of it which make a genuine function of it: as for example, in the attempt to express 'a exists' by 'For some x, x is identical with a'.

if any one of the set is a tautology, but otherwise a contradiction. That is, it is a tautology if x and y can take different values (i.e. if there are two individuals), but otherwise a contradiction.[1] He concludes that the series 'There is one individual. . . . There are at least 2 individuals. . . . There are at least n individuals . . .' begins by being tautologous; but somewhere it begins to be contradictory, and the position of the last tautologous term shews the number of individuals.

Now Wittgenstein rejected propositions of the form 'There is not an x such that $x \neq x$', jeering at it with the remark: 'Would this not be true if "there were things" but these were not identical with themselves?' (5.5352). He did not regard identity as a genuine function. But the point can be made without using identity. Let us suppose, for the sake of simplicity, that there are only two objects, a and b, and one function, f. Then the possibilities fa, ~fa, fb, ~fb, will be all the possibilities that there are. Suppose that we write these possibilities down as follows:

(1) There are an x and a y and a ϕ such that ϕx and ϕy
(2) There are an x and a y and a ϕ such that ϕx and ~ϕy
(3) There are an x and a y and a ϕ such that ~ϕx and ϕy
(4) There are an x and a y and a ϕ such that ~ϕx and ~ϕy.

These are *all* the possibilities; therefore, the 'complete description of the world in a completely generalized proposition', of which Wittgenstein speaks at 5.526, will be given by one of them.

Here we have 'described the world' without any preliminary correlation of a name with a particular object. And then, in order to arrive at the usual way of putting it, in which names are used, we need only add e.g. 'x is a, and y is b, and ϕ is f'. But *that* this is a complete description, i.e. is all the facts there are, can only be expressed if we can add such propositions as 'and there are not an x and a y and a z, and there are not a ϕ and a ψ such that . . .'. Hence it is required at 5.526 that we should have propositions stating: 'There is one and only one x such that . . .', which would have to be of the form: 'There is an x and there are not an x and a y, such that . . .'.

This surely means that the 'complete description in completely

[1] Ramsey, *The Foundations of Mathematics*, pp. 59–60.

generalized propositions' would, in the finite case, consist partly of existential propositions employing *more* variables than there are names of distinct objects. But if what *is* false *can be* true, then the completely generalized propositions will allow more play to the facts than the totality of elementary propositions. Yet at 5.5262 Wittgenstein denies this: 'The truth or falsehood of *every* proposition alters something about the general structure of the world. And the play which is allowed to its structure by the totality of elementary propositions is just that which is limited by the completely general propositions.'

This conclusion can only be avoided by adopting Ramsey's suggestion and saying that the series of propositions

$$(Ex,\phi)\phi x \vee \sim\phi x$$
$$(Ex,y,\phi)\phi x \vee \sim\phi x.\phi y \vee \sim\phi y$$
$$(Ex,y,z,\phi)\phi x \vee \sim\phi x.\phi y \vee \sim\phi y.\phi z \vee \sim\phi z$$

etc., would go over, in the finite case, from being tautologies to being contradictions at the point at which the number of different name variables employed exceeded the number of different names. And it is really only in the finite case that Wittgenstein's theory can be expounded with much clarity.

I find this conclusion unsatisfactory: in the infinite case, Wittgenstein's theory can hardly be explained at all: we have to take the finite case and say that he saw no important difference between it and the infinite case; while in the finite case the view seems to lead to a sudden transition of an *existential* proposition from tautology to contradiction.

Did not Wittgenstein resist any attempt to symbolize 'The universe is not empty' in 'There are things', regarding these as 'pseudo-propositions' attempting to *say* what *shews*? At 5.535 he says that what the 'Axiom of Infinity' (which says that there is an infinite number of objects) is supposed to mean 'would be expressed in language by there being infinitely many names with different references'.

If (Ex)fx is the logical sum: 'fa v fb v fc . . .' then (Ex)fx v ~fx is the logical sum of the singular tautologies: fa v ~fa v fb v ~fb v fc v ~fc . . .; and so $(Ex,\phi)\phi x \vee \sim\phi x$ will be the logical sum of all the singular tautologies: fa v ~fa v fb v ~fb . . . ga v ~ga v gb v ~gb

. . . etc. In these propositions, then, we can see how 'the existence of things' is something 'shewn' and not said. But if Wittgenstein allows $(Ex)\phi x . \sim(Ex,y)\phi x.\phi y$ as a way of saying that *only* one thing has ϕ, as he does at 5.5321, it is difficult to see how he could avoid a way of admitting formulae which say 'There are *only* n things and m functions' without using either 'thing' or 'function' as a function.

12

KNOWLEDGE AND CERTAINTY

Probably the best-known thesis of the *Tractatus* is that 'metaphysical' statements are nonsensical, and that the only sayable things are propositions of natural science (6.53). Now natural science is surely the sphere of the empirically discoverable; and the 'empirically discoverable' is the same as 'what can be verified by the senses'. The passage therefore suggests the following quick and easy way of dealing with 'metaphysical' propositions: what *sense-observations* would verify and what falsify them? If none, then they are senseless. This was the method of criticism adopted by the Vienna Circle and in this country by Professor A. J. Ayer.

There are certain difficulties about ascribing this doctrine to the *Tractatus*. There is nothing about sensible verification there. If Wittgenstein means to suggest that we can test a proposition for significance by seeing if we can state the sense-observations that would verify it, then it is surprising that he does not say so. Nor is a reference to sensible verifiability immediately implicit in the identification of 'what can be said' with 'the propositions of natural science'; for the totality of natural science has been defined earlier in the book (4.11) as the totality of true propositions. Nowhere have we any suggestion of a general method for criticizing sentences, according to which we may say: 'What observations would verify (or falsify) that? If none, then it does not mean anything.' Such a general method for criticizing sentences would obviously need a preliminary justification; and it is difficult to see how the *Tractatus*, for example, can be taken as such a preliminary justification, when it says nothing about sensible observation.

The general method that Wittgenstein does suggest is that of 'shewing that a man has supplied no meaning [or perhaps: "no reference"] for certain signs in his sentences'. I can illustrate the method from Wittgenstein's later way of discussing problems. He once greeted me with the question: 'Why do people say that it was natural to think that the sun went round the earth rather than that the earth turned on its axis?' I replied: 'I suppose, because it looked as if the sun went round the earth.' 'Well,' he asked, 'what would it have looked like if it had *looked* as if the earth turned on its axis?' This question brought it out that I had hitherto given no relevant meaning to 'it looks as if' in 'it looks as if the sun goes round the earth'. My reply was to hold out my hands with the palms upward, and raise them from my knees in a circular sweep, at the same time leaning backwards and assuming a dizzy expression. 'Exactly!' he said. In another case, I might have found that I could not supply any meaning other than that suggested by a naive conception, which could be destroyed by a question. The naive conception is really thoughtlessness, but it may take the power of a Copernicus effectively to call it in question.

Different philosophers have meant different things by 'metaphysical'. Kant also attacked metaphysics: but Kant would not have called 'Every rod has a length', or 'Time is one-dimensional and has only one direction', metaphysical in the sense in which he attacked metaphysics; whereas for Wittgenstein they are so.

The criticism of sentences as expressing no real thought, according to the principles of the *Tractatus*, could never be of any very simple general form; each criticism would be *ad hoc*, and fall within the subject-matter with which the sentence professed to deal. For example, if someone says that time moves only in one direction, we investigate this by asking him what processes he is comparing.

One frequently used tool in such enquiries is: 'What would it be for it to be otherwise?'—when, e.g. someone has said: 'Time has only one direction.' Here we are asked for an intelligible description of a state of affairs in which the asserted proposition—let it be, say, 'the future comes *after* the past'—does *not* hold. As far as sensible verification is concerned, the asserted proposition and the alternative to it that is being asked for are, or may be, on the same level;

the relation of actual sense-experiences to each is not necessarily being investigated. What is operative here is evidently not a sensible-verification theory, but the picture theory of the significant description: both the proposition and its negation are supposed to describe a possibility, otherwise the status of the proposition is other than that of a significant description.

'Psychology is no more akin to philosophy than any other natural science. Theory of knowledge is the philosophy of psychology' (4.1121). In this passage Wittgenstein is trying to break the dictatorial control over the rest of philosophy that had long been exercised by what is called theory of knowledge—that is, by the philosophy of sensation, perception, imagination, and, generally, of 'experience'. He did not succeed. He and Frege avoided making theory of knowledge the cardinal theory of philosophy simply by cutting it dead; by doing none, and concentrating on the philosophy of logic. But the influence of the *Tractatus* produced logical positivism, whose main doctrine is 'verificationism'; and in that doctrine theory of knowledge once more reigned supreme, and a prominent position was given to the test for significance by asking for the observations that would verify a statement. (Further, in the period between the *Tractatus* and the time when he began to write *Philosophical Investigations*, Wittgenstein's own ideas were more closely akin to those of the logical positivists than before or after.)

We can see how the *Tractatus* generated logical positivism, although the two philosophies are incompatible, by studying Moritz Schlick's essay, *Meaning and Verification*: 'Whenever we ask about a sentence, "What does it mean?" what we expect is instruction as to the circumstances in which the sentence is to be used; we want a description of the conditions under which the sentence will form a *true* proposition, and of those which will make it *false*.' Here Schlick seems to follow the *Tractatus*, except in the last clause of his statement: the *Tractatus* says that I 'determine the sense' of a proposition by 'determining in what circumstances I call it true' (4.063). (It is implicit in this that the 'circumstances' in question may hold or not hold; for it is an essential part of the picture theory that a proposition which held in *all* circumstances would not have 'sense': it would lack TF poles.)

Schlick calls the 'description of the conditions' under which a word has application, or a sentence is true, the 'rules for the use' of the word or sentence. These 'rules' will consist partly of 'ostensive definitions', of which the simplest form will be a pointing gesture combined with the pronouncing of the word; this can be done with words like 'blue'. For words like 'immediate', 'chance', 'because', 'again', Schlick says, the ostensive definition is of a more complicated kind: 'in these cases we require the presence of certain complex situations, and the meaning of the words is defined by the way we use them in these different situations.' All rules for use 'ultimately point to ostensive definitions'. 'This,' Schlick says, 'is the situation, and nothing seems to me simpler or less questionable. It is this situation and nothing else that we describe when we affirm that the meaning of a proposition can be given only by giving the rules of its verification in experience. (The addition "in experience" is really superfluous, as no other kind of verification has been defined.)'[1]

This shews us the transition from the *Tractatus* to 'verificationism' very clearly. What Schlick says leads immediately (a) to the quick test for significance: 'What experience would verify this?' and (b) to the maintenance of theory of knowledge as the cardinal theory of philosophy.

In the *Tractatus*, the 'determination of the circumstances in which I call a proposition true' must be a statement of its truth-conditions. This is a completely different thing from a 'rule for the use' of a sentence, if this takes the form of an 'ostensive definition'. There could be no statement of the truth-conditions of an elementary proposition, other than a restatement of it; and for all non-elementary propositions there can always be statements of truth-conditions. If, then, Schlick is following the *Tractatus*, 'ostensive definition' can only be relevant to the elementary proposition.

Further, Schlick insists that our 'rules for use' are 'arbitrary'; we give what rules we like; all that is essential is that we give some. The only arbitrariness in the *Tractatus* is in the assignment of names. There is no arbitrariness about the fact that a certain type of arrangement of names is capable of representing such-and-such a

[1] Moritz Schlick, *Meaning and Verification*, reprinted in Feigl and Sellars, *Readings in Philosophical Analysis*.

situation; it can do that only by reproducing in its own structure the arrangement of objects in the situation, and we cannot *make* it do so at will. Therefore, on the *Tractatus* view, there is no room for criticizing a sentence on the ground that we have not stipulated what situation it describes; but only on the ground that we have not assigned a reference to some of the words in it. The utterance of a sentence in a context in which it is true does not take the place of a stipulation of truth-conditions; the most that it can do is to shew someone the reference of the words; he will then understand the propositional sign, in its positive or negative sense, by meaning the objects named in it. Then 'you have said something meaningless' could only mean 'you have not assigned a reference to *this* expression', and never 'you have not shewn what observations would establish the truth of this'.

On the *Tractatus* view, then, one could not ask what observations would establish the truth of a proposition unless the 'structures' of possible observation statements already stood in certain internal relations to the 'structure' of the proposition. In the presence of these internal relations, the question of meaningfulness cannot arise, except in the form of a question about the reference of the individual signs; if these signs are not given a reference, the proposition could not be 'given' a sense, even by stipulating that its truth would be established if and only if such-and-such observation statements were verified. An alleged 'proposition' that was so 'given a sense' would necessarily be, not a proposition, but the simple sign of a complex; and then the sentences in which the 'proposition' occurred would have to stand in internal relations to the 'observation statements'; these internal relations would then supply us with the description of a complex, and the definition of a simple sign for that complex; and the 'observation statements' would give the truth-conditions of propositions in which that sign occurred. This doctrine is quite different from Schlick's.

In *Philosophical Investigations*, where Wittgenstein makes an extensive investigation of psychological concepts, his object was to shew that it is not necessary to introduce the problems of epistemology of—i.e. of perception, imagination, and generally of 'experiencing'—into the discussion of other problems of philosophy. That is to say, we can discuss e.g. the problems implicit in the expression 'the process of time', without laying foundations by giving an account of the ways in which we apprehend time—memory, expectation, experience of succession, and so on.

Knowledge and certainty, however, *are* topics for the philosophy of logic. In doing logic we are not indeed interested in what is the case, or in what things are certainly known, or in the conditions for certainty in practice. But logical theory must allow for the certainty of propositions which are not logically necessary. Otherwise logic would have no application. For 'It is clear in advance that the logical proof of a significant proposition and proof *in* logic (i.e. proof of a logical proposition) must be two quite different things. The significant proposition asserts something, and its proof shows that it is so' (6.1263, 6.1264). Thus the proof of a significant proposition is not hypothetical. If its proof proves that it is the case, it is presupposed that those propositions from which it is proved are known to be true; for if they were uncertain, the conclusions would be equally uncertain. The only 'certainty' would then be hypothetical—that if the premises are true the conclusion is; but that is not what Wittgenstein calls a significant proposition; it is a proposition of logic, and proof of it nothing but a 'mechanical expedient to facilitate the recognition of it as a tautology' (6.1262). Thus, if we are to speak of proving significant propositions, 'A knows p' cannot be an ideal form of description without specifiable instances, nor one exemplified only in 'knowledge' of tautologies.

It is easy to misunderstand certain remarks in the *Tractatus* which have to do with this question and to suppose that Wittgenstein calls *only* tautologies certain. At 4.464 he says: 'The truth of tautology is certain, that of a proposition is possible, and of contradiction impossible. (Certain, possible, impossible: here we have a hint of that gradation which we need in probability theory.)' And at 5.525: 'Certainty, possibility or impossibility of a state of affairs are expressed, not by a proposition, but by an expression's being a tautology, a significant proposition or a contradiction.' It would be natural at first sight to take these remarks as implying that certainty belongs only to tautology. But the 'state of affairs' *whose certainty is expressed by an expression's being* a tautology cannot be a state of affairs *described by* a tautology; for Wittgenstein is insistent that tautology describes no state of affairs—is true for every possible state of affairs (4.466). Again the 'significant proposition asserts something, and its proof shows that it is so'; but there will be no such proof if certainty belongs only to a tautology.

Now if we take the hint given by the parenthetical remark at 4.464 and examine the theory of probability as it is described by the *Tractatus*, we find that the first impression perhaps conveyed by these propositions is mistaken, as it must be if Wittgenstein is consistent.

The account of probability is closely connected with the view that all the propositions are truth-functions of elementary propositions. At 5.15 we are told: 'If T_r is the number of truth-grounds of the proposition "r", T_{rs} the number of the truth-grounds of the proposition "s" which are at the same time truth-grounds of "r", then we call the ratio $T_{rs}: T_r$ the measure of the *probability* given by the proposition "r" to the proposition "s"' (5.15). That is, if we assume 'p' and 'q' to be elementary, since 'p or q' has 3 possible combinations of the truth-values of 'p' and 'q' which make it true, and only 1 in common with 'p and q', the measure of the probability given by 'p or q' to 'p and q' is 1:3.

This account of probability has been criticized as resting upon the arbitrary dogma that all elementary propositions are equally probable. 'Two elementary propositions give one another the probability ½' (5.152). Now Wittgenstein also says: 'Propositions which have no truth-arguments in common with one another, we call independent of one another' (5.152). This is not an author's 'we'. Turning it round we might say: 'When we speak of propositions as independent of one another, what this really means is that they have no truth-arguments in common, i.e. are truth-functions of quite separate sets of elementary propositions.' With this we get some light on what is meant by saying 'the *application* of logic decides what elementary propositions there are' (5.557). That is to say: if in the *application* of logic—i.e. reasoning not 'in logic' but from facts—we (rightly) say 'even if *this* is so, *that* would not have to be so, it is not even made probable, they have nothing to do with another': then we have found propositions that are truth-functions of quite separate sets of elementary propositions. But he goes on to say at this place: 'Logic cannot anticipate what resides in its application' and 'Logic and its application must not overlap.' Thus the question what are the elementary propositions does not belong to logic at all.

These passages shew the doubtfulness of part of Wittgenstein's criticism of the *Tractatus* in *Philosophical Investigations*. He jeers at the idea that when I say 'The broom is in the corner' I really mean 'The broomstick is in the corner and so is the brush and the broomstick is stuck in the brush.' But I shall recognize the negation of any of those propositions as constituting an objection to 'The broom is in the corner'; and that is all that the *Tractatus* theory requires. If I understand a proposition, I shall know what more detailed statements are inconsistent with it; these will then be more elementary than it is.

To return to the probability theory: 'If p follows from q, then the proposition "q" gives the proposition "p" the probability 1. The certainty of the logical conclusion is a limiting case of probability' (5.162). This can readily be seen from the *Tractatus* account of probability together with its account of inference, according to which what follows from a proposition is already stated by it (5.14–.141).

Now, however, we are in a position to understand the proposition: 'Certainty, possibility, or impossibility of a state of affairs is expressed not by a proposition, but by an expression's being a tautology, a significant proposition, or a contradiction.' Since an expression that is a tautology (or contradiction) does not answer to any 'state of affairs', what expresses the certain (or impossible) 'state of affairs' *itself*, as opposed to expressing its certainty (or impossibility), will not be the tautologous (or contradictory) expression, but rather one of the propositions that occur as components of this tautology (or contradiction). Moreover, in order to get 'a hint of that gradation which we need in probability theory', 'possibility' must here be taken as excluding *both certainty and* impossibility. Take a case where 's' is a significant proposition and 'r' expresses something we know. Then the 'state of affairs' expressed by 's' will be certain if 'r.∼s' is a contradiction (i.e. if 'r⊃s' is a tautology); it will be impossible if 'r.s' is a contradiction (i.e. if 'r⊃~s' is a tautology); it will be, relative to our knowledge, merely 'possible' if 'r.s' and 'r.~s' are *both* significant propositions (*each* of them must be *either* a significant proposition *or* a contradiction, if 'r' and 's' are both significant propositions).

This raises the question how we know that r; does the same account apply as would apply to 's' if it were 'certain' that s, and does this go on indefinitely, or do we come to a stop somewhere? Wittgenstein's view is at this point obscure; but he refers to 'being completely acquainted with a fact' (5.156), and presumably held that here we do come to a stop.

Thus Wittgenstein offers an extraordinarily over-simplified account of knowledge, which would presumably have to be filled out with an account of 'acquaintance with facts'. 'A knows p', he remarks at 5.1362, 'is senseless if p is a tautology.' (We should notice that the word is 'senseless', not 'nonsensical'; that is to say, the knowledge that p, when 'p' is a tautology, is treated as he treats the truth of 'p'.) But he has just said that the connection between knowledge and what is known is that of logical necessity. He is not referring to the mere fact that 'A knows p, but p is not true' is a contradiction; but to his theory, which would be the foundation for that fact, that the certainty of a state of affairs comes out in an expression's being a tautology. That is to say, if A knows p, then, for some q, the fact that q is a fact that A is 'acquainted' with, and q⊃p is a tautology.

The remark: 'Certainty, possibility and impossibility of a state of affairs are expressed, not by the proposition but . . .' stands as a comment on 'It is incorrect to give "fx is possible" as the verbal rendering of (Ex)(fx), as Russell does.' Russell held that necessity, possibility (contingency) and impossibility belong, not to propositions, but to propositional functions, such as 'fx'. ' "fx" is necessary', he says, means that all values of fx are true.[1]

In the passage we have been considering, Wittgenstein discusses not necessity, possibility and impossibility, but certainty, possibility and impossibility. This might seem insignificant, from his saying

[1] *See* e.g. the final paragraph of a chapter 'Propositional Functions' in Russell's *Introduction to Mathematical Philosophy*.

'the truth of tautology is certain'; but, as we have seen, he cannot hold that *only* the truth of tautology is certain. His objection to Russell's account of necessity (and hence of logical impossibility) is made elsewhere, at 6.1231: 'The mark of logical propositions is *not* general validity. For to be general only means: to be accidentally valid for all things. An ungeneralized proposition can be tautologous just as well as a generalized one.'

'That precedent,' Wittgenstein concludes 5.525, 'to which one would always like to appeal, must reside in the very symbol itself.' He evidently refers to a reason why it is especially tempting to equate '(Ex)(fx)' and 'fx is possible'. The most fundamental motive for adopting Russell's views is that it would be one way of getting rid of the puzzling character of 'necessary', 'possible' and 'impossible'; Wittgenstein has his own way of doing that. There remains, however, the feeling that a *case* will guarantee possibility, and thus give the assertion of possibility a sense, as nothing else could; this is like the lawyer's feeling that the best way of showing a procedure to be legal is to cite a precedent for it. So Russell thought that 'fx' is possible only if there is an *actual* case of an f.

Now Wittgenstein acknowledges this desire for 'a precedent', but says that this precedent resides in the symbol itself. The 'symbol itself' will be the significant proposition. For 'in the proposition a situation is as it were put together experimentally' (4.031). It is as if the construction of small models of mechanisms were used to make reports on what machines there were in some place, and one also constructed hypothetical models, say in order to ask whether there are any of these in that place. If the models are in clay and do not move, one might want to know what makes them express possible hypotheses. But if the models are themselves working mechanisms, the 'precedent' to which one would want to appeal would be in the models themselves. And so it is, Wittgenstein says, with *significant* propositions.

No 'precedent' is to be found in tautology and contradiction; Wittgenstein's remark has sole application to significant propositions. For 'sentences which are true for every state of affairs cannot be connections of signs at all, for otherwise only particular connections of objects will correspond to them. (And there isn't any logical combination to which there corresponds *no* combination of the objects.)' (4.466). To regard tautologies (logically necessary propositions) as descriptions is as if one were to regard the empty space where the mechanism was to go as itself a model—for all possible mechanisms. But the significant proposition is a *logical working model* of the situation it asserts to exist.

13

'MYSTICISM' AND SOLIPSISM

When Russell received the MS. of the *Tractatus* from Wittgenstein, then in an Italian prison-camp, after the First World War, he wrote some comments and questions. Presumably he laid great stress on the account of logical propositions as tautologies; his letter is not extant but we know he attached great importance to Wittgenstein's researches on this subject from a footnote in his *Introduction to Mathematical Philosophy*. In reply he received a letter from Wittgenstein saying:

> 'Now I'm afraid you haven't really got hold of my main contention, to which the whole business of logical propositions is only corollary. The main point is the theory of what can be expressed (*gesagt*) by propositions—i.e. by language (and, what comes to the same, what can be *thought*) and what cannot be expressed by propositions, but only shown (*gezeigt*); which, I believe, is the cardinal problem of philosophy. . . .'

We have seen what 'can be said' according to this theory: that, and that only, 'can be said' the negative of which is also a possibility, so that which of the two possibilities is actual has to be discovered by 'comparing the proposition with reality'. This notion is rather vague, but it is clearly implied that the comparison does not consist in mere thought: 'there is no picture that is true *a priori*'. That is to say, if a proposition has a negation which is a perfectly good possibility, then it cannot be settled whether the proposition is true or false just by considering what it means. The locus of direct 'comparison with reality' lies in the facts we are 'acquainted with';

if so, then, on Wittgenstein's theory of inference, we can have no knowledge of significant propositions that is not a restatement (or an 'abstract'—5.156) of propositions known by 'acquaintance' to be true. (This theory of knowledge has, to be sure, nothing but clarity and simplicity to recommend it.) As for tautologies and contradictions, they are devoid of 'sense' and 'say nothing'.

But an important part is played in the *Tractatus* by the things which, though they cannot be 'said', are yet 'shewn' or 'displayed'. That is to say: it would be right to call them 'true' if, *per impossibile*, they could be said; in fact they cannot be called true, since they cannot be said, but 'can be shewn', or 'are exhibited', in the propositions saying the various things that can be said.

Now the things that would be true if they could be said are obviously important. Can we then draw a distinction between things that are 'shewn', and things the opposite of which is 'shewn'; between the things that would be true if they could be said, and those that would be false if they could be said? It is impossible to speak like this of attempted contradictions of what 'is shewn', as we have already seen in a trivial case: whereas ' "Someone" is *not* the name of someone' is intended to say something 'quite correct' (as Wittgenstein says of solipsism), we must say concerning ' "Someone" *is* the name of someone' that what such a proposition intends is not merely not correct, but quite incoherent and confused; the demonstration that this is so completely destroys the idea that there is anything at all behind the would-be statement. Nevertheless there are utterances which at least sound like attempts to say the opposite of the things that are 'quite correct' in this sense; and there will be more error, or more darkness, in such attempts than in trying to say the things that are 'shewn', even if they are really unsayable.

It would presumably be because of this that Wittgenstein regards the sentences of the *Tractatus* as helpful, in spite of their being strictly nonsensical according to the very doctrine that they propound; someone who had used them like steps 'to climb out beyond them' would be helped by them to 'see the world rightly'. That is to say, he would see what 'is shewn', instead of being down in a bog confusedly trying to propound and assert sometimes cases of what is 'shewn', sometimes would-be contradictions of these.

This idea of philosophic truth would explain one feature of philosophy: what a philosopher declares to be philosophically false is supposed not to be possible or even really conceivable; the false ideas which he conceives himself to be attacking must be presented as chimaeras, as not really thinkable thoughts at all. Or, as Wittgenstein put it: An *impossible* thought is an impossible *thought* (5.61)—and that is why it is not possible to say what it is that cannot be thought; it can only be forms of words or suggestions of the imagination that are attacked. Aristotle rejecting separate forms, Hume rejecting substance, exemplify the difficulty: if you want to argue that something is a philosophical illusion, you cannot treat it as a false hypothesis. Even if for purposes of argument you bring it into contempt by treating it as an hypothesis, what you infer from it is not a contradiction but an incoherence.

We must distinguish in the theory of the *Tractatus* between logical truths and the things that are 'shewn'; logical truths, whose character we have already discussed, are the 'tautologies', and are '*sense-less*' propositions (lacking TF poles), their negations being 'contradictions'; attempts to say what is 'shewn' produce '*non-sensical*' formations of words—i.e. sentence-like formations whose constituents turn out not to have any meaning in those forms of sentences—e.g. one uses a formal concept like 'concept' as if it were a proper concept (Chapter 7, pp. 111–12). Here the attempt to express what one sees breaks down.

The connection between the tautologies, or sense-less propositions of logic, and the unsayable things that are 'shewn', is that the tautologies shew the 'logic of the world'. But what they shew is not what they are an attempt to say: for Wittgenstein does not regard them as an attempt to say anything. They are, however, legitimate constructions, introduced into the system of propositions as 0 was introduced into the system of numerals. Nor are they the only propositions which 'shew' anything, or which shew 'the logic of the world': on the contrary, every proposition at least does that.

Of all the things that are unsayably 'shewn', the most prominent in the *Tractatus* is this 'logic of the world' or 'of the facts'. 'My most fundamental thought is this: logical constants are not proxies for anything. The logic of the facts cannot have anything going proxy for it' (4.0342). Here he is contrasting logical constants with names, which 'go proxy' for their objects: 'The possibility of sentences,' he has just said, 'rests upon the principle of signs as going proxy for objects'—and what this principle in turn amounts to is the possibility of logical picturing through one fact's having the same logical form as another—for only in the context of the proposition will a sign go proxy for an object.

Sentences thus cannot represent, and nothing in them can stand for, 'the logic of the facts': they can only reproduce it. An attempt to say what it is that they so reproduce leads to stammering.—This view does seem to be true. I once bought toffees with the names of the flavours, 'treacle', 'Devon cream' and so on printed on the papers, and was momentarily startled to find one labelled 'fruit or nut'. It cannot be 'fruit or nut', I said; it's fruit or it's nut! Any attempt to say what the truth-functional constants like 'or' mean must fail; we can only shew it.

Or again; if asked to explain the composition of the simplest statement, we say that this word means, or refers to, such-and-such, and this one means such-and-such, and together they mean that . . . (or: someone who puts them together makes the statement that . . .) —and there follows just such another composition of signs as we were trying to explain.

Again, if we try to explain the essence of a relational expression to ourselves, we reproduce the relational form in our explanation. For, as we have seen, we must make the distinction between 'aRb' and 'bRa'; and if we do this by e.g. saying that in one the relation goes from a to b, and in the other from b to a, we produce a sentence which employs the essential relational form; for it reproduces the distinction produced by exchanging the places of the terms.

All the logical devices—the detailed twiddles and manipulations of our language—combine, Wittgenstein tells us at 5.511, into an infinitely fine network, forming 'the great mirror'—that is to say, the mirror of language, whose logical character makes it reflect the world and makes its individual sentences say that such-and-such is the case. The simplest and most characteristic mark of this is that we do not have to learn the meanings of all the sentences of our language; given the understanding of the words, we understand and construct sentences, and know what they mean without having it explained to us.

It is essential to see that logic does not describe any facts: that there are no logical facts. It was at one time natural to think that the field of logic was the field of what was *a priori* true, i.e. true independently of all existence. On this Wittgenstein says at 5.552: 'The "experience" that we need to understand logic is not that something is thus or thus, but that something *is*: but that is not an experience. Logic precedes any experience—that something is *thus*. It comes before the *How*, not before the *What*.' According to the *Tractatus* the 'what' is conveyed by the simple names, which cannot be taken to pieces by definitions (3.261) and which name the 'substance of the world' (2.0211). Thus even when a simple name is replaced by a definite description, the description is merely 'about' the object, it could not 'express' it (3.221).

From this, it is clear that Wittgenstein held that what was given by experience was always facts; a grasp of the 'substance of the world', which we shew we have in being able to describe the facts we experience, is not given by any experience. For of any experience it can be asked what it shews as being the case; since this can be the case or not, indifferently, its being the case cannot possibly tell us anything about logic. For everything logical about a (significant) proposition is understood before it is known whether the proposition is true or not.

But logic cannot be thought of as something quite independent of the world either. For then 'How could we apply logic?' (5.5521). That is to say, if logical truth were there without any world, then when there was a world, how could it be said: such-and-such cannot be, because there is a logical fact that is inconsistent with it? 'It could be said: If there would be such a thing as logic, even if there were no world, then how can there be such a thing as logic, when there is a world?' (i.e.: if logic comprised facts that the facts in the world had to be consistent with, then logic would no longer be logic, for it is logic that judges of the consistency of facts.) 'It has been said that God can create everything but what is contrary to the laws of logic.—The point is, that we could not *say* what an "unlogical" world would be like' (3.031). So the medieval philosopher says that God, to whom no 'word' is impossible, yet cannot change the past, because 'change the past' is not a 'word'.

Thus when the *Tractatus* tells us that 'Logic is transcendental', it does not mean that the propositions of logic state transcendental truths; it means that they, like all other propositions, shew something that pervades everything sayable and is itself unsayable. If it were sayable, then failure to accord with it would have to be expressible too, and thus would be a possibility.

I will now consider the most notorious of the things that Wittgenstein says are 'shewn', but cannot be said: the truth of solipsism. I am a solipsist if I think: 'I am the only *I*: the world, including all the people in it, is essentially an object of experience, and therefore of *my* experience.' Wittgenstein says: what is intended here is right, but it can't be said. (5.62).

It is a fairly natural thought that 'where there is consciousness, there is an I'; but this raises immediate questions both about 'consciousness', and about the legitimacy of speaking of '*an* I'. If one considers examples of consciousness, as it is being approached here, one does not think of how e.g. one can see that someone is now *conscious* (he was, say, asleep before); but rather of contents of consciousness, such as pain, images, the visual field; and what is there *to* the consciousness except the pain, the image, or the visual field itself? The essential thing is that these are being considered 'from inside'; all that there is from outside corresponding to these words is manifestations of them in words and behaviour.

So it comes out that it is illegitimate to speak of '*an* I'. 'From inside' means only 'as *I* know things'; I describe those things—something, however, I cannot communicate or express: I try to, by saying I speak 'from an inside point of view'. But there is no other *point of view*. Suppose others too speak of the 'inside point of view'? That is *my* experience or *my* supposition of spoken words.

In a later writing Wittgenstein imagined a convention whereby some individual, A, is used as a centre for the language of experience and thought in the following way: Everyone says 'There is pain', or 'It thinks', when A is in pain, or is thinking; for other people the locution would be, say, 'X is behaving as A behaves when there is pain etc.' Now, he said, if I am the centre, this language has a peculiar but quite inexpressible advantage over the languages in which other people are taken as centres. It is inexpressible, because if I try to express it in the language with myself as centre naturally my statement, as coming from the person who is the centre, is specially related to the language that has me as centre; and if I try to express it in a language with someone else as centre, then the description, in that language, of the alternative possible language with me as centre gives it no special position in comparison with any other alternative language. But all these languages correspond, and one and the same reality corresponds to them all and to the 'physical language'.

This passage, though written some years after the *Tractatus*, appears very close to it in thought. For that 'advantage' was absolute. Thus I *am* the centre, but this is inexpressible.

In the *Tractatus* Wittgenstein speaks of 'my language' (5.6) and explains this as meaning 'the only language that I understand'[1] (5.62). Its limits 'stand for the limits of my world'. I cannot postulate a language for talking about the relation of language, the world, and the philosophical I, in which my world (the world given by the limits of my language) would be one particular thing to talk about. I can only say how things are in the world corresponding to my language. But this manifests the 'all-comprehending world-mirroring logic'.

That is why, having said at 5.6 'The limits of my language mean the limits of my world', Wittgenstein gives as the first comment on this pronouncement a number of remarks on logic: 'Logic fills the world: the limits of the world are also its limits' (5.61). The argument is: 'The limits of my language mean the limits of my world; but all languages have one and the same logic, and its limits are those of the world; therefore the limits of my world and of the world are one and the same; therefore the world is my world.'

[1] The emphasized definite article shews that 'der Sprache' in 5.62 means '*that* language' making a back reference which must be to 'my language' in 5.6.—In the first edition of this book I translated the parenthesis in 5.62 'the language that only I understand'. But Dr. C. Lewy has found a copy of the first edition of the *Tractatus* with a correction by Wittgenstein giving 'the only language that I understand'.

But the 'I' of this way of talking is not something that can be found as a mind or soul, a subject of consciousness, one among others; there is no such thing to be 'found' as the subject of consciousness in this sense. All that can be found is what consciousness is of, the contents of consciousness: 'I am my world' and 'The world and life are one'. Hence this 'I', whose language has the special position, is unique; the world described by this language is just the real world: 'Thoroughly thought out, solipsism coincides with pure realism' (5.64).

It is not possible to understand this passage unless one has a good deal of sympathy with solipsism. We should remember that Wittgenstein had been much impressed by Schopenhauer as a boy; many traces of this sympathy are to be found in the *Tractatus*. Probably no one who reads the opening of *The World as Will and Idea*: 'The world is my idea', without any responsiveness, will be able to enter into Wittgenstein's thought here.

Mrs. Ladd Franklin is reported to have written to Bertrand Russell saying that she was a solipsist and could not understand why everyone else was not too! It is possible that the comic effect was intentional, and the joke on her side. The necessity of solipsism is very arguable; why should a solipsist not argue it with everyone capable of arguing? Nothing would follow, even if two solipsists exchanged views with mutual congratulation, about any cession by either to the other of the unique position he conceives for himself. If two people discuss Descartes' 'Cogito', they can agree that 'This is an argument I can administer to myself alone,' and each can hold the other would be incorrect to have disputed that; if snow fell in appropriate sentences, one could dispute, agree and disagree with, those sentences.

Further, it is very difficult to think of ways out of solipsism. Indeed solipsism is often held to be irrefutable, but too absurd to concern oneself with. In Wittgenstein's version, it is clear that the 'I' of solipsism is not used to refer to anything, body or soul; for in respect of these it is plain that all men are alike. The 'I' refers to the centre of life, or the point from which everything is seen.

It is difficult to get rid of such a conception once one has it. One may well want to do so; e.g. one may feel that it makes the 'I' too godlike. 'What is history to me? Mine is the first and only world!' Wittgenstein wrote in his notebooks on this theme, and: 'There are two godheads: God, and the I.' (He did not follow Schopenhauer in saying: 'The world is my will'; on the contrary: 'The world is independent of my will—and anything's being as I want it is a "grace of fate".' (6.373-4). 'Hence,' he wrote in his notebooks, 'the feeling of being dependent on an alien will.')

It is not altogether easy to understand Wittgenstein's idea of 'the limit'. It too is partly derivative from Schopenhauer, who wrote of it as follows:

> 'Any one percipient being, with the object, constitutes the whole world as idea just as fully as the existing millions would do; but if this one were to disappear then the whole world as idea would cease to be. These halves are therefore inseparable even for thought, for each of the two has meaning and existence only through and for the other, each appears with the other and vanishes with it. They limit each other immediately.'

Again, Schopenhauer remarks on the fear of death that it is really the fear of losing the present, and says that this is like being afraid of slipping down the sides of the globe, as someone might do who did not realize that the top is wherever he is.

The idea of the world as having *limits* which philosophy displays to us appears over and over again in the *Tractatus*. It is perhaps best known in the dictum of 6.45: 'The view of the world *sub specie aeterni* is the view of it as a—limited—whole. The feeling of the world as a limited whole is the mystical feeling.' The world 'as a limited whole' is not suddenly introduced here as a new topic. We encounter the world conceived as a whole—as *all* that is the case—and as limited—namely by being all that is the case—at the very outset of the book; the feeling of the world as a whole appears in the remark at 1.2: 'The world splits up into facts', for it is only of a whole that we can say it splits up.

'Mysticism' is a rather odd name for what Wittgenstein is speaking of; in popular language it suggests extraordinary and unusual experiences, thoughts and visions peculiar to an extraordinary type of individual; and no doubt it has been taken in that sense, and written off, the more easily because Wittgenstein was himself well known to be an extraordinary individual—the very man to have some mysticism about him. But Wittgenstein took the term over from Russell, who used it in a special way, with reference to an entirely ordinary feeling; one that is well expressed at 6.52: 'We feel that even if all *possible* scientific questions have been answered, still the problems of life have not been touched at all.' And his further comment on this is: 'Of course there then just is no question left, and just this is the answer.'

This comment can be taken in two ways: First, Wittgenstein might be saying—and this is what Professor Ayer, for example, would make of his remarks—that people who have wanted to say what the meaning of life consisted in have had nothing in them but a lot of nonsense. This cannot be the right interpretation; for he speaks of people 'to whom the meaning of life has become clear'. But he says of them that they have not been able to say it. Now such people have not failed for want of trying; they have usually said a great deal. He means that they have failed to state what they wished to state; that it was never possible to state it as it is possible to state indifferent truth. He probably had Tolstoy especially in mind, whose explanations of what he thought he understood are miserable failures; but whose understanding is manifested, and whose preaching comes through, in a story like *Hadji Murad.*

Wittgenstein's idea is probably made clearest at 6.41: 'The meaning of the world must lie outside the world. In the world everything is as it is, everything happens as it does happen; there is no value *in* it—if there were any, it would have no value. If there is a value that has value, it must lie outside all happening and outside being this way or that. For all happening and being this way or that is accidental. What makes it non-accidental cannot be found in the world, for otherwise this thing would in its turn be accidental.' And: 'God does not reveal himself *in* the world' (6.432)—i.e. it is not in things' being this way as opposed to that that God is revealed.

This follows from the picture theory; a proposition and its negation are both possible; which one is true is accidental. Why then, having said that whatever is the case is accidental, does Wittgenstein speak of 'what makes it non-accidental'? To understand this, we have to understand what he says about the will. The most important remark that he makes here is: 'The facts all belong to the task set, and not to the solution' (6.4321). '*Aufgabe*', which I translate 'task set', is the German for a child's school exercise, or piece of homework. Life is like a boy doing sums. (At the end of his life he used the analogy still.) Now the reason why the solution cannot bring in any facts is that it is concerned with good and evil; and the good or evil character of what is good or evil is non-accidental; it therefore cannot consist in this happening rather than that, for that is accidental.

In doing one's task, one receives certain laws, of the form 'Thou shalt . . .' This, Wittgenstein says, prompts the question: And suppose I do not do it? 'But it is clear that ethics has nothing to do with punishment or reward in the ordinary sense.' Still 'there must be something right about that question. There must be a kind of ethical reward and ethical punishment, but these must reside in the action itself. (And it is also clear that the reward must be something pleasant and the punishment something unpleasant)' (6.422).

Now what is 'the action itself'? Wittgenstein insists that 'the world is independent of my will; there is no logical connection between will and world'—no logical connection between my will and what actually happens at all. In so far as an event in the world can be described as voluntary, and volition be studied, the will, and therefore action, is 'a phenomenon, of interest only to psychology'. Therefore 'action', in the ethical sense, is something independent of what happens; and this is the bearer of good and evil. Thus the 'will that is the bearer of the ethical' (6.423) belongs among the transcendentals of the *Tractatus*, along with the mystical and the meaning of life. The connection of will with the world is that 'the facts' belong to the task one is set. If one has reached a solution, this is made to be a solution, not by any alteration of the facts that may have taken place—any such alteration, even if one intended it, is accidental and merely a 'grace of fate'—but by an alteration 'in the limits of the world' (6.43).

It is this part of the *Tractatus* that seems to me most obviously wrong. As Wittgenstein asks in *Philosophical Investigation* (§644):

'Did not your intention [of which you are ashamed] reside also in what you *did*?' 'What happens' includes 'actions', in the sense of the word in which 'good' and 'bad' are predicated of actions. But the philosophy of the *Tractatus* could not allow this to be so; hence the chimerical 'will' which effects nothing in the world, but only alters the 'limits' of the world. In his notebooks Wittgenstein entertained some more reasonable considerations, which are closely akin to his thought in *Philosophical Investigations*; and then rejected them, in the following revealing passage:

> 'The consideration of willing makes it look as if one part of the world were closer to me than another (which would be intolerable). But, of course, it is undeniable that in the popular sense there are things that I do and other things not done by me. In this way, then, the will would not confront the world as its equivalent,[1] which must be impossible.'

The true philosophical account of this matter has still to be found; saying that the *Tractatus* is obviously wrong here, I do not wish to suggest that I know what is right.

There is a strong impression made by the end of the *Tractatus*, as if Wittgenstein saw the world looking at him with a face; logic helped to reveal the face. Now a face can look at you with a sad or happy, grave or grim, good or evil expression, and with more or less expression. And so he speaks of the world 'waxing or waning as a whole', i.e., in terms of my analogy, as having more or less expression, or a good or evil expression. The world thought of, not as how things are, but as *however* they are—seen as a whole—is the matter of logic; thought of as my life, it is the matter of ethics; thought of as an object of contemplation, the matter of aesthetics:

[1] The contrast with Schopenhauer, as well as the kinship, is interesting. Schopenhauer thought that 'the world is my will' and is bad; and that the only redemption for the will is 'to turn and freely deny itself'. Wittgenstein thought that the world is good and independent of my will; good and bad willing are attitudes to the world as a whole. The goodness of the world, however, is not anything in *how* it is, but in its being at all; and lies outside all being-this-way-or-that. The good will therefore will not be concerned with how things are, and in that sense is like Schopenhauer's good will.

all these, then, are 'transcendental'. Many years later, in a 'lecture on Ethics', Wittgenstein wrote: 'If I want to fix my mind on what I mean by absolute or ethical value, it always happens that one particular experience presents itself to me which is therefore in a sense my experience for excellence[1] . . . the best way of describing it is to say that when I have it *I wonder at the existence of the world.*' The identification of ethics and aesthetics (6.421) comes about in this way: good and bad willing changes the world only as the object of contemplation as a whole.

The man, however, who having been helped by the *Tractatus* 'sees the world rightly', i.e. sees what logic reveals as 'shewn', will not attempt to say it, since he knows it is unsayable. As for how much advantage it is to him, Wittgenstein makes no great claim; in the Introduction he said: 'The whole meaning of the book could perhaps be summed up as follows: What can be said at all can be said clearly, and what cannot be spoken of we must be silent about.' But his final judgment on the value of the book was this: 'It shews how little has been done, when these problems have been solved.'

[1] Wittgenstein's English is bad here. He means: 'The experience which I think of when I want to remind myself what I mean by *excellence*.'

FURTHER READING

WITTGENSTEIN, L. *Philosophical Investigations*; Blackwell, Oxford, especially Part I, §§1–116.

Remarks on the Foundations of Mathematics; Blackwell, Oxford, Part I.

Notebooks 1914–16; Blackwell, Oxford.

FREGE, G. *Translations from the Philosophical Writings of Gottlob Frege*; Blackwell, Oxford.

The Foundations of Arithmetic; Blackwell, Oxford.

RUSSELL, B. *The Principles of Mathematics*; Allen & Unwin, London, especially Chapters III–V and VII.

The Problems of Philosophy; Home University Library.

Logic and Knowledge; Allen & Unwin, London, especially 'On Denoting' and 'The Philosophy of Logical Atomism'.

Introduction to Mathematical Philosophy; Allen & Unwin, London.

RAMSEY, F. P. *The Foundations of Mathematics*; Routledge, London.

BASSON AND O'CONNOR. *Introduction to Symbolic Logic* (2nd edition); University Tutorial Press, London.

QUINE, W. V. O. *Methods of Logic*; Routledge, London.

HILBERT AND ACKERMANN. *Mathematical Logic*; Chelsea Publishing Co., New York.

VON WRIGHT, G. H. *Logical Studies*; Routledge, London, I.

INDEX

R

S

T

V

W